THROUGH
the
GROVES

THROUGH
the
GROVES

A Memoir

ANNE HULL

Henry Holt and Company
New York

Henry Holt and Company
Publishers since 1866
120 Broadway
New York, New York 10271
www.henryholt.com

Henry Holt® and ⓗ® are registered trademarks of
Macmillan Publishing Group, LLC.

Library of Congress Cataloging-in-Publication Data is available.

ISBN: 9780805093377

Our books may be purchased in bulk for promotional, educational,
or business use. Please contact your local bookseller or the Macmillan
Corporate and Premium Sales Department at (800) 221-7945, extension
5442, or by e-mail at MacmillanSpecialMarkets@macmillan.com.

First Edition 2023

Designed by Meryl Sussman Levavi

Printed in the United States of America

1   3   5   7   9   10   8   6   4   2

For Victoria Desmond
and John Hull

THROUGH
the
GROVES

CHAPTER 1

A dirt road took us there. When we reached the grove, the Ford hesitated, as if sizing up the chances of a square metal machine penetrating the round world of oranges.

"Hold on, Sister," my father said, shifting gear.

His CB radio antenna whipped in the air like a nine-foot machete. It caught in the tree branches and bent backward, then THWACK. Leaves and busted twigs rained down on us inside the car. Pesticide dust exploded off the trees. And oranges—big heavy oranges—dropped through the windows like bombs.

"Look out for Bouncing Betties!" Dad yelled when one hit the front seat.

Slats of raw sunlight bore down through the shade of the trees as the dirty beige Ford moved through the flickering movie. My father studied each tree we rolled past, glaring at it with suspicion, looking for all the ways it might be trying to trick him. He let the car steer itself as he tore the cellophane off a new pack of Winstons.

It was the summer of 1967 and he had just started his new job as a fruit buyer for HP Hood, the juice processor. He was supposed to make sure Hood got the best quality oranges and grapefruit for juice production. After he bought the citrus from growers, he had to keep the trees healthy until the fruit was ready to be picked, and then he had to ensure that the truckloads of citrus arrived at Hood's juice house on time.

"The variables out to defeat a man are many," he said, exhaling smoke. "Bugs, drought, freezes, aphids, red mites, canker, labor problems."

Neither of us said anything for a while.

Sweat trickled down the side of my father's face as he brooded. He was six feet and lanky, loose-limbed, with one hand draped over the steering wheel and perspiration coming through his white oxford shirt.

"How old are you, anyway?" I asked. I had just turned six.

"Your old daddy is twenty-eight," he said.

His dashboard was covered in cigarette ash and pesticide dust. Dead bug skeletons were down along the windshield, piles of them, crispy as croutons, and every time a breeze hit, they lifted up in midair before settling back down. My father's attention was out his window, on the Valencia orange trees. Valencias were juicers and soon to be in cartons in grocery stores if the variables didn't defeat Hood's new man in the field.

We crept along at three miles an hour. All of a sudden, he hit the brakes.

"Stay in the car," he said, stalking off with his magnifying glass. I kept an eye on him as I unwrapped the bacon sandwich my mother made for me. He held his magnifying glass over some leaves, Sherlock Holmes–style.

My mother had given me lots of instruction. Don't talk too much. Don't pester the man with questions. Drink plenty of water. Speak up if I need to use the bathroom.

A bathroom! Of all the misinformed advice. So far that day the closest I saw to a bathroom was a tar paper shack next to an irrigation ditch. When I had to go, Dad reached under his seat for a roll of toilet paper. "Take this," he said. Two rows over, I squatted in the sand, holding a stick for snake protection.

"Best not to shatter all your mama's illusions by telling her every detail," Dad said when I got back in the car.

Withholding confidential information from my mother— how exciting. I was obsessed with spy craft. Dad helped me with my correspondence to the cereal companies of Battle Creek, Michigan, mailing away for Captain Quisp decoder rings, invisible ink, and secret compartment watches. Whatever I owned that was worth owning came from Battle Creek. Dad and I would sit at the kitchen table together in the evening and think of reasons why I was qualified to own the tools of espionage.

I'd noticed the box of test tubes rattling on his back seat. I asked him why he needed test tubes with stoppers. He said Hood required him to test juice samples for sugars and acids. I could see the test tubes were unused. None of the seals were broken. That didn't seem right. "Are you going to get in trouble for not testing the juice?" I asked.

He said he preferred what he called the old-fashioned taste test. I would watch him do it a hundred times that summer. He stood by a tree with his pocketknife, cut a hole into the orange, and sucked the juice out. He held it in his mouth for a few seconds, calculating the juice into yields, pallets, and truckloads, then spat into the dirt. He had his answers.

My father gave me one rule to follow: don't touch the glove box. "Understand?"

Whenever he left me alone in the car, I opened the glove box. It let out a puff of scent, like dirty pennies. Inside was a pistol. I moved it aside to examine the rattlesnake kit. The small briefcase of death was at the back of the glove box. Military lettering stamped on the box said: "Mine Safety Appliances Company." That was just to throw off interested parties. The clasp of the rattlesnake kit popped open. Inside, the miniature surgical instruments were strapped down—tourniquet, suction cup, and a lancet covered in creased white tissue.

MY FATHER'S territory was the citrus-growing region of Central Florida known as the Ridge. It ran a hundred miles from north to south, from up around Clermont straight down to Lake Placid. It wasn't a large area but in the 1960s the Ridge had the heaviest concentration of citrus groves in the world. One botanical grid after another, dark green regiments of trees marching up and down the middle of the state. We lived at the bottom of the Ridge in a town called Sebring.

In spring when the orange blossoms opened, it was like God had knocked over a bottle of Ladies of Gardenia. The smell was so strong it burned into my hair and clothes, and the dog's fur. The blossoms heaved and sighed for three weeks straight, and just as they started to fade the cooking houses started processing fruit for juice. For ten hours a day, the cook houses pumped caramelized smoke into the air that smelled of spun brown sugar.

Once we'd gone to Jacksonville, three hours north of the Ridge, a paper mill town on the St. Johns River. When that rotten-egg breeze came rolling off the river, it left me gasping in the back seat, dazed by the realization that the world could stink. I was glad we weren't in paper. I was glad we were in oranges.

IF THE history of Central Florida were charted out on a graph, it would start with primordial sludge and then curve toward the Paleo Indians, the Calusa Indians, the Tocobaga Indians, Ponce de León, runaway slaves, snuff-dipping white settlers, the US Army, Osceola, the great Seminole warrior, malaria, cattle, citrus, and a dull heat that left it undesirable for much besides oranges until the early 1960s, when Walt Disney took a plane ride over the vast emptiness, looked down, and said, "There."

The interior of Central Florida was so desolate that my father kept a gallon of water and a box of Saltines in his car. He said you could eat all the oranges you wanted, but good luck if you needed a flush toilet or a pay phone. He also said it was no place for a child, though Disney was betting otherwise.

Florida's other citrus-growing region was much smaller, east of the Ridge, along the coast, and it was called Indian River. The Indian River people did a better job marketing their fruit, rhapsodizing about tidal Indian breezes that rang like poetry in the Yankee ear. Their fruit was prettier to look at because each piece of fruit was buffed out to the shine of a Cadillac.

On the Ridge, we didn't mind if an orange left your hands dirty as long as juice dripped down your chin. Plus, we had more groves, wall-to-wall.

The competition was from California, though it was hardly a contest. The unremitting heat and humidity on the Ridge made our citrus exceptional juice bombs. What had started to pose a threat was a variety coming out of California called the seedless clementine. It was a no fuss version of the

Florida tangerine, which was loaded with seeds. Dad said it might ruin us for good.

MY FATHER regularly had one citrus problem or another gnawing at him. A lower demand for navel oranges. Ortho raising the price on pesticide. He chewed so much Dentyne gum during that one that he cracked a molar.

The seedless clementine seemed a threat of a higher magnitude.

One day my father and I were parked in a grove while he talked about it with the other citrus men on the CB radio. One said that the clementine could knock out 25 percent of our citrus business. Dad listened, jotting down numbers on a pad of paper, crop yield versus net sales. George LaMartin's voice cut through the ear-busting static. He and Dad were the same age, but George cussed more.

George said America was going to hell in a handcart if people were too lazy to spit out a few goddamn seeds.

The crackle and scratch started to drown out the voices. "Go to 32!" someone said, before they lost each other. Switching channels, they met back up on 32 and kept talking.

Astronauts were constantly flying overhead in Florida in those days, but the citrus men hardly bothered to look up. Nothing took their focus from the oranges. The moon was not an orange. The moon was a fad. Citrus was king and it would last forever.

LOOKING OUT my father's windshield, I was seeing things I would never see again. Places that weren't even on maps, where the sky disappeared and the radio went dead. Whole towns were entombed in Spanish moss, with gnarled branches of live oaks and blackjacks strangling each other in the tannic darkness. We rumbled past old pioneer settlements rotting in the humidity. Black creeks wound like tangled snakes. Birds spread their skeletal wings but never flew off. When it seemed we might not ever see daylight again, the road deposited us into blinding sunlight.

Dad's fruit-buying territory for Hood crossed over four counties, or about four thousand square miles of rural land and unmarked roads. He had maps in the car, seven or eight of them, but I'd yet to see him consult one. When he came to a cattle gate with a yellow rag tied to the middle rung, that's where we turned left. He didn't disparage maps, but I got the feeling from him and the other citrus men that freestyle navigating was a point of pride. He also favored the "back way" or the "old way." Old Highway 98 or Old Highway 64, we were always on Old Something.

One day we passed a group of men clearing brush on the side of the highway. They had chains attached to their ankles. They moved slowly, dragging their leg irons as they scythed through the tall grass in the ditches. Just in front of them was a truck that crept along and a guard on back holding a shot-gun next to a watercooler.

As we passed the shackled contingent, some of the men looked up. Their faces were slick with sweat. Dad said it was impolite to stare at the prisoners. I turned back around in my seat but watched them in the rearview mirror until they were a speck and gone. My father scrounged in his shirt pocket for a Winston, probably trying to think of a parable about the uneven justice of captivity. Instead, he asked if I knew any chain gang songs.

> *The hobo told the bum*
> *If you got any cornbread, save me some.*

We sang it together a couple times. It made me thirsty, thinking of the cottony insides of the prisoners' mouths and the water truck they'd never reach.

Every Friday we had a car full of money. Dad paid the labor crews on Friday afternoon, so first thing in the morning we went to the bank in Sebring. It was ice-cold and brand-new, and our teller looked like Jeannie C. Riley who sang "Harper Valley P.T.A." She counted out a thick stack of bills that she put into a leather bank pouch and slid toward Dad. Out on the road we were Bonnie and Clyde. It was my job to hold the bank pouch.

"Would you mind keeping this safe for me?" Dad had said. He also took his gun out of the glove box and put it under his seat.

Knowing the money was going to orange pickers, the bank teller must have dug into her drawer for the most beat-up money she could find. The bills were greasy and thin, defaced with scrawling—Masonic symbols, Halloween bats, and the Egyptian eye, or devil horns on Abe Lincoln. The messages people wrote were in large block letters that spelled out HELP ME!!!! Or, PLEASE CALL LAMAR AT AVON PARK CORRECTIONAL. From going through the bank pouch and studying the money, I learned the word "pussy" and the first two lines of John 3:16.

As abused as that currency was, my father said it worked fine. You'll see.

Most of the pickers knocked off for the summer, working other jobs, but there were still plenty who were fertilizing, watering, hoeing, and disking. My father didn't pay each individual laborer; he paid their crew chief, Booker Sanders.

We found Booker in one grove or another by spotting his truck. It was a heap, like a pile of scrap metal someone abandoned in the hot sand.

"Well, Booker, another week," my father said, after they shook hands.

Booker was an oak tree in bib overalls. His forearms were scarred with cross marks from picking oranges. The branches were stiff and sharp, daring any human to reach in and snap off a piece of fruit. Some of the fruit hung beautifully at the outer edges, but much of it was inside the tree, and this meant the picker's face and neck would be slashed as he leaned into the middle of the tree. Booker's arms spoke to his years picking oranges until he finally moved up to manage a crew of his own.

He was at least fifteen years older than my father, a deacon at Zion Hills Missionary Baptist, and so thoroughly networked that he fixed up the white people in town with domestic help, lawn men, and citrus workers. But his gift and genius was citrus. Dad said Booker had a ten-key adding machine in his head and reams of spreadsheets that mere mortals could not keep up with.

Under different circumstances, Booker Sanders would have been the mayor of Sebring or owned ten thousand acres of groves and cattle. In his current circumstances as a Black man in 1967 rural Florida, his role was to cede authority to the less knowledgeable white man in charge.

Dad handed the payroll cash to Booker and watched

Booker count out the grimy bills on the hood of the Ford. After that, Dad said he wanted to show Booker a grove that was nearby.

"Get in the car, Booker. I'll carry us over there," Dad said.

"I'll take my truck," Booker said.

"Well, I need to show you where it is," Dad said, standing at the open door.

"I know where it is," Booker said, getting in his truck.

Dad got in the car and we followed behind Booker.

By four o'clock that afternoon, the bank pouch was empty. The cinder block taverns blinked to life and men at the gas station ripped into ten-pound bags of North Pole ice for their coolers. The sagging grocery store was suddenly a madhouse of wire buggies trundling out with pork shoulders and collards. Dad and I watched the payday fever through the windshield.

Of all the days in the week, Friday was the day my mother most wanted me to ride with Dad. My presence was supposed to keep him from succumbing to the Friday afternoon fever. With me in the car, he'd steer clear of the red neon Schlitz signs that called to him on his drive home. The bar didn't even have to be on a map, but he knew where it was, based on animal instinct for red neon signs. A bar could be a half mile off the main road, next to an abandoned turpentine camp and hidden by moss, and he'd somehow end up there. My mother's hopeful logic that a child might act as a human shield against this intuition was worth a try.

BEFORE MY father took the job with Hood, he was a spray man for Ortho chemical company, selling pesticides to smaller growers on the south end of the Ridge. One day he was out in the field when he saw a Dalmatian on the side of the road. The dog was starved and wandering in a ditch. Dad brought him home, and we named him Ortho.

The job with Hood was a tall rung up the ladder; you could tell by the business cards they made for him. They came in a small ivory box and Dad pulled the lid off so my little brother Dwight and I could take turns sniffing the fresh smell. He'd given us each a business card. I put mine in my cigar box, where I kept his chewed-up pencils stamped with "Florida Spray Man's Association." I planned on bringing the pencils to first grade, imagining the splash it would make with my classmates to flaunt the backing of a trade group.

The new job came with a lot more responsibility and pressure. When he described it to my mother, who didn't know a tangelo from a tangerine, he said, "It's the whole enchilada."

The afternoon he signed the contract, we celebrated by going to a steakhouse on the highway. I had always wanted to go. Once a month on payday, my parents went there by themselves, and the next morning, my mother would fry the steak scraps in butter for my breakfast.

My father promised to take me with them some day and said I could even order a Roy Rogers.

My mother whipped around from the stove, thinking I was too young to be introduced to the charms of cocktails— even one without alcohol in it. "John!" she said, giving my father the eye.

"What's a Roy Rogers?" I asked, suddenly desperate for one.

She turned back to the frying pan. "A Roy Rogers is a

children's drink in an adult glass," she said, making it sound like the most boring thing ever invented.

THE MAIN road in and out of town was US 27, a four-lane highway pounded thin by two-ton trucks hauling oranges. It had all the good things—steakhouses, shrimp joints, cocktail lounges with air-conditioning.

At night the neon signs blinked on and electric buckets of chicken started to spin overhead, casting colored lights out in the darkness. In the morning when the sun came up, you could see the truth of the situation. About fifty thousand Valencia orange trees had just doglegged around a few CHAR-BROIL signs.

It was still daylight when we went, and the parking lot of the steakhouse was filling with cars and boat trailers. The boats leaked water from the lake. The side cocktail lounge vibrated with sound, and we went into the steakhouse. The AC unit high in the corner was blowing as hard as it could. Dad asked for a booth.

When the waitress came over, Dad gestured toward me. I had waited so long to say it: "A Roy Rogers, please."

After my Roy Rogers, I had a second Roy Rogers. My father had the waitress running back and forth between the cocktail lounge and our table all night. My mother hardly touched her dinner.

Finally, she got up and followed the waitress. Whatever she said made the next drink not come.

Dad didn't notice; he was too busy telling us stories. My favorite was about the cattleman who trained his bantam rooster to walk out to the road and bring in the mail. We stayed in the booth a long time until my mother said, "John, give me the keys."

The next morning the door to my parents' bedroom stayed shut. Their voices were hushed; I couldn't make out what they were saying. Every now and then one of the grim-faced negotiators would come out for coffee or a new pack of cigarettes; then it was back to their deliberations.

Later that day, they asked me to come into the kitchen. My father was at the table working the crossword puzzle. My mother was at the counter dredging okra in a paper bag, shaking it like a maraca as little puffs of white flour escaped. She kept shaking the maraca as if whatever she wanted wasn't that urgent, but she cut her eyes toward my father. He didn't look too good, and the pencil in his hand seemed jumpy. He waited for my mother to begin. She made her voice sound nonchalant. They had an idea that I might like to go to work with my father a couple days a week and keep him company. My mother cast it as a summer adventure. "Just you and Dad," she said.

It didn't occur to me to ask either of my parents why a six-year-old would accompany a grown man to work; I was too swept away in the adventure.

THE JUNE night before our first day, my mother had come into my room with a shopping bag from Grant's variety store. She must have stopped on her way from work. Inside was a new thermos. It was tartan plaid, like a Junior Girl Scout might take to Camp Dorothy Thomas for a night of ghost stories and s'mores. My mother stood in the doorway of my room after she'd switched out the light. She stayed there for a while, looking down at the floor where my boots and thermos were lined up for the morning.

By the end of the first week, we must have put seven hundred miles on the Ford. I never knew which days I would ride with Dad. I was roused for duty at 6 a.m. and I went along. We rode with all four windows down, the wind so loud we had to shout like pilots. To keep his business papers from flying around, my father used a grapefruit as a paperweight. He acted like it was the most natural thing in the world to be accompanied by a child associate.

At each stop, he introduced me to the growers, pesticide men, and fertilizer brokers who populated his territory.

I had never seen such a reptilian assemblage of humanity. The whites of the men's eyes were seared bloody red by the sun. Their faces cracked when they smiled. Cancer ate away at their noses. They hawked up wet green balls of slime that came from years of breathing in pesticide as they sprayed the groves with five-gallon containers of malathion strapped on their backs. No one used respirators back then. The wind pushed the poison back in their faces, filling their lungs and covering their skin. When the chemicals made them nauseous and dizzy, they took a break for a while, then got back to it.

One afternoon we went to see a man in a trailer next to some groves. The trailer was his office, and he kept it as cold as a meat locker for his breathing. Dad warned me, but when we climbed the steps of the trailer in the noon heat and opened the door, the air was so cold it stung my face. The man had a friendly face, but he wheezed like an accordion.

"John," he said to my father, "you got you a little helper with you today?"

"I certainly do," my father answered, smiling. There was

no chair for me, so I sat in the corner on top of some old phone books while a stream of contagions from the wall unit AC splashed on my legs. The man had two items on his desk, an adding machine and a Maxwell House coffee can. He worked the ten-key without looking. Every so often he reached for the coffee can. Right before he bowed his head into the can, he glanced at me apologetically and said, "Scuse me, gal." Then he hawked up another gob. He'd be dead in ten years.

Compared to these ravaged creatures my father looked like a newborn. Impervious to the elements, he wore a cotton shirt every day, long sleeves buttoned at the wrist, no matter that it was burning hot in summer. His skin was tan and smooth and unlined. His wavy brown hair was shiny as an otter's. He breathed normally. Whatever had happened to those other men had not yet happened to him.

I sat in the corner chewing stick after stick of Dentyne. I sharpened pencils and sketched nocturnal landscapes of Gemini astronauts soaring over the orange groves. When every item had been explored, all that was left was the fruit calendar nailed to the back of the wood-grain door. Each month featured a different succulent creature—a Valencia, a honeybell, a Parson Brown. A secret calendar was tucked behind the citrus calendar. It was also chockablock with succulent creatures but not a Parson Brown among them.

"Hey, Dad," I said, wanting to show him my find. Right away I was sorry I did.

The meeting ended shortly thereafter. I waited for the scolding as we walked to the car, but instead my father kept his eyes on the ground. First thing my father did was flip on the CB to tell his cohorts that the foot-washing Baptist at such and such packing house had a nudie calendar in his office! He laughed so hard he folded over in a coughing fit. Mischief revived him.

WHENEVER HE wanted to share a confidence with me, he dropped his voice low and spoke solemnly, as if the forthcoming secret was a revelation of great significance and I was old enough to handle it.

Take the story about Harold Avery, an old grower in Fort Drum. As a young pesticide salesman, Dad told me, he had called on the old man. He lived in an ancient lean-to house you could knock down with a rock. His brogans were tied on just one side and he wore overalls, their straps tied crossways. He showed my father the grove, with its eaten-up fruit. Dad's magnifying glass revealed mites.

The old man eyed him cautiously. Then he pulled a soiled check from his pocket along with a stub of a pencil. The old man said, "How soon can you deliver?"

My father wrote up the order for pesticides.

Mr. Avery got down over the hood of the car like he was praying and scrawled out the check.

He said, "You know, Mr. Hull, I haven't asked no one for nothing. I worked on a boat that dredged the St. Lucie canal. What I made on poker, I saved for this land."

Then he handed Dad the biggest order of his life, and the two shook hands.

Ten minutes down the road, it occurred to Dad that the check might not be good. The nearest pay phone was in Yeehaw Junction, forty minutes away. Dad got his boss on the line and said he might have just been taken by a grower named Harold Avery, and unfortunately Dad had promised he would deliver the pesticide. A long silence followed.

His boss said, "That check is good for any amount Mr. Avery wrote it for."

This was the part of the story where Dad's voice dropped low, recounting what his boss told him.

"John, I don't worry about these orange people," the boss said. "Tomato people are different. But a man who owns his own trees, he's got credit because he's good for it. That's how people in oranges do."

We were orange people. He was talking about us.

ONE MORNING I started feeling not so good. The asphalt was scorching and the sun burned through the windshield, and the horizon started to swirl. It happened fast. Vomit was all over the front seat.

"Son of a BITCH," my father half yelled, having little familiarity in the area of child vomit. I started crying. After pulling over to clean me off with a rag, he said a Coke might help, and we barreled off in search of carbonation.

Twenty minutes later, we were pulling into an abandoned gas station. Grass was coming up through the concrete and the tires stacked out front looked like they belonged to Model Ts. Dad drove around back and parked in front of a wooden door that was standing open. Cobwebs hung down in the blackness. It looked like a haunted house with a toilet and a sink. I washed myself off in the rusty water and when I came out my father walked around to the front of the gas station. I followed him inside.

"Well, I'll be damned," said a voice. An actual man was sitting behind the counter. Ancient bags of pork rinds and ladies' travel-size rain bonnets were strung on fishing tackle over his head. From somewhere he produced a cold bottle of Coke. My father directed me to a greasy chair. An hour later I was still sitting there.

God almighty, my father could talk. There were periods of silence, where neither he nor the other man said a word. They stared at an oil spot on the floor. "Well," one or the other said, and then the conversation started up again.

When we did finally get up to leave, Mr. Pork Rinds seemed sad to see us go.

"Wait a minute now," he said. Just as he had produced a cold bottle of Coke from a junk pile, he reached into a glass jar with a red lid and pulled out a moon pie. It was for me. He said he did not know when he would see the next customer and certainly that customer would not be as enjoyable as we were.

After my father pulled back onto the road, I turned around to look at the gas station. The white building with green trim seemed like an apparition in the blinding sun. All around it was an enormous blue sky. But I knew a man was in there.

ANOTHER DAY, we rode somewhere south of Sebring. "What kind of grove is that?" Dad asked, gesturing with his cigarette. The trees were dark green and picked clean of oranges. I couldn't tell one grove apart from the next.

"This reminds me of Clyde Connolly," Dad said.

"Who's Clyde Connolly?"

"Clyde Connelly was one of my first customers when I started with Cal Spray," Dad said, relaxing back into his car seat. "A twenty-four-year-old know-nothing greenhorn pesticide salesman calling on one of the most prosperous growers on the Ridge."

Clyde had a big spread near Lake Placid. A spread and a Baby Bell helicopter.

"Now, I had never flown before," Dad said, "Not in a plane or a helicopter. But Clyde asked, 'John, how about you and I go up for a ride?'"

Soon they were sweeping over dark green patterns of citrus. "Clyde knew I wasn't too sharp on my fruit yet," Dad said, tipping his cigarette in the wind. "He'd get at 150 feet and he'd just park it above the trees and we'd study the fruit."

When lunchtime came Clyde flew to a café that was bordered by live power lines. He struggled to set the helicopter down. Diners came out to the parking lot to watch. Dad could see only grim squinting faces down below. He worried that California Spray would have to call my mother to tell her she was a widow. Clyde eventually got them down. Dad was so relieved to be alive he told the waitress to put lunch and pie on Cal Spray, even though he didn't have an expense account.

OVER THE days in the groves, we developed a rhythm. When he started the engine, it was time to go. That was the signal. Get in the car, Sister. We drove to our next stop, the dirty oranges rolling around on the floorboards. I wore cowboy boots, hot and sockless and not the carved kind I wanted but good enough for groves.

Dad took a laissez-faire attitude toward my tomboy ways, an attitude that fewer and fewer people seemed willing to extend. He didn't care if I balled my shirt up and stuck it down in the front seat. He bought me my own pair of silver nail clippers like the ones he carried in his trouser pocket. We sat in the middle of a grove with all four doors of the Ford flung open to get a breeze, listening to the CB radio as we clipped our nails.

We often went through the phosphate town of Bartow. Bartow was as scorched and treeless as the moon, yet in the midst of that gypsum-covered town was a Royal Castle. What a shock, seeing the small glass diner with orange counter stools in the middle of a lunar landscape. The milkshake cups were decorated with crowns. I rinsed out my straws and saved them in my cigar box at home. My father liked Royal Castle, too, and we stopped there frequently.

The gypsum stacks were on either side of the car. They were five stories high like snowy Kilimanjaros, ready to devour children who could not resist climbing them. Neither guard dog nor chain-link fence installed by the phosphate companies could stem the tide of climbers, Dad said. Every time we passed the white mountains, he took the opportunity to remind me of the danger. He told me about the one boy who was buried alive. Each time, he added a new detail to reinforce the danger.

I'd picture the boy's shoes flying off in the cascading tonnage; his eyes, wide open, which had to be cleaned out at the morgue. It didn't seem like the boy's story could get any worse, but it always would.

"And the sad thing was, all the money he saved for the fair was in his pocket," Dad would say.

SOME DAYS, he hardly talked. He smoked and ruminated, with pinpoints of perspiration on his forehead as he drove in silence. Other times he talked nonstop, unspooling stories about his family's early days in Central Florida. I'd look out the window, the landscape blurring past. There was something about hearing a story in a car.

My favorite was about his great-grandmother, Mollie. As a girl, she and her father took their wagon to Tampa to sell vegetables. It was a two-day ride to get there and Mollie held a rifle across her lap. They camped for the night at Six Mile Creek, where they barely slept a wink for fear of Indians. Just as I was getting my mind around Mollie holding her rifle as dawn broke and pushing the horses on toward Tampa, my father shook his head.

"What?" I'd ask.

"Don't forget that was just one way," he'd say. "They had to get back home to Hopewell, too, again."

HIS FAMILY came to Florida in the 1860s, arriving in a covered wagon from Georgia. This would have been J. W. Hull, a solemn man with a six-inch beard and a wife named Nancy. The federal government had been steadily deporting or killing Indians in Central Florida for decades, offering the confiscated land at cut-rate prices to lure new residents to the state. J. W. and Nancy Hull spent a few years in North Florida growing oranges before moving south to Hillsborough County, where they joined a small group of other like-minded Baptists who were trying to establish a settlement. Palmetto scrubs choked the land and slashed their skin. The ground squished underfoot. The humidity was so oppressive that mules dropped dead in their harnesses. Without a hint of irony, the settlers named their new home Hopewell.

For the Hulls, God and oranges were the cornerstone of life. Until a church was built, they stomped off into the pines for the camp meetings. They sat on sticky sap benches for hours so a preacher could yell at them on their one day off.

In the killer freezes of 1894 and 1895, the entire citrus industry of Florida was wiped from the map overnight, nearly every grove destroyed, and more than four million boxes of fruit killed on the trees.

At Hopewell, Dad's family planted new groves and successive generations tended the trees and refused to budge from the original homestead that over time became a magnificent spread of land. Until my father moved sixty-five miles south to Sebring, no one had ever ventured so far from Hopewell.

Dad was different from his cousins who stayed behind. They tended the groves; he told stories about people who tended the groves. I could see how different they were when we visited Hopewell. His cousins reached for their sweet tea with hands like rawhide. My father's hands were soft on the underside. His grandmother and great-grandmother showed a special tenderness for him. They'd roll out biscuits for him or dredge chicken-fried steak, or in Big Nanny's case, open her big ledger-style checkbook.

He was courteously deferential to these women, but he was that way with everyone. He also had a melancholic streak a mile wide. When I sensed it, I ran out in the yard to play.

He had a nervous habit of doodling stick figures hanging by a noose. I used to find the ominous sketches on the front cover of the phone book, on notepads; any scrap of paper was a canvas for a stick figure dangling on a hanging post. When I asked him about it, he said he'd been playing hangman by himself. Putting a hand gently on my shoulder, he asked incredulously, "You mean you've never heard of One Man Hangman?"

I was 95 percent sure there was no such game but not 100 percent sure.

By the second month in the Ford, a feeling of captivity set in. It was August, and in a few weeks I would start first grade. I did not want to spend my last days of summer stuck in the hot car.

"Quit your bellyaching," my father said. He was no longer the congenial tour guide and had stopped regaling me with stories.

Now he was giving me all the crap jobs, like cleaning off the lovebugs that splattered against the windshield of the Ford. In late summer, the hot muggy air was so thick with lovebugs you couldn't leave your mouth open for even a second. The Ford was literally oozing with lovebug slime because the slow-drifting black flies did most of their copulation midair. It was never just one lovebug that smashed into the car; it was the pair, by the hundreds.

On the last day I rode with my father, we pulled into a gas station to use their water hose. He took the windshield and told me to start on the grillwork.

"Use this," he said, handing me a kitchen pot holder. It was red and white, with a strawberry appliqué. The pot holder was one of his aunt Dot's signature handicrafts.

"But that's Aunt Dot's," I said, clutching the pot holder.

With his back turned to me, the heat coming up off the blacktop asphalt and down from the colorless sky, my father asked if he needed to remind me that we don't have to report every single thing that goes on.

I cleaned the car. The water that came out of the hose at the gas station was so hot it burned my hand.

Nothing about that day went right. We cruised through Bartow again, past the white gypsum mountains where the little boy had been buried alive. My father's eyes were fixed on the road, the ash from his cigarette about to blow all over us.

"Dad," I said, over the wind, "who got the fair money in that boy's pocket?"

My father sat up, as if a trance had been snapped. He tipped his ash in the wind. "Well, I imagine his mother and daddy," he said.

As usual, Royal Castle called to us from up the road.

"Would you like a hamburger?" my father asked. My hand was already on the door handle.

The oniony breeze blew across us at the outside walk-up window. Flies circled in and out of the window, which was halfway closed. A man wearing a white paper hat appeared. He leaned down and turned his face sideways to talk to us, as if it didn't occur to him to raise the window. My father gestured toward me. He thought children should place their own orders as soon as they were old enough to read. When it was my father's turn, he said he didn't believe he'd be having any lunch.

We drove on, something diminished between us. We went a long way in near silence.

At the next grove, he started up the rows. It was bouncy and rough. He was driving faster than usual and when he took a sandy turn, I was pushed against the door. In the middle of the grove, he stopped. Just cut the engine. He told me to reach in back for his stomach medicine. While he chugged from the bottle of Pepto-Bismol, he listened to the CB radio, flipping from one frequency to the next. I decided to go for a walk.

Next to the grove was a cow pasture. The cows looked up in their cross-eyed way and continued chewing, mindless of the egrets that perched on top of their backs. There were hundreds of these white scavenger birds in the pasture and a lone gnarled cypress tree that had been struck by lightning. Every Florida pasture looked the same.

I was walking along, not paying much attention to anything, when a thunderous WHOOSH broke the silence. All at once, the white birds lifted from the pasture. Hundreds of them, spooked and flapping around in confusion before falling into formation and moving off into the low sky.

I ran back to the car. The birds' sudden flight scared me.

My father was turning the CB radio off. The empty Pepto-Bismol bottle was on the back seat. He was screwing the cap back on a different bottle. Breathlessly, I told him about the white birds. He said the CB radio was full of chatter about a sonic boom. Everyone speculated it was probably construction work on the Disney park.

"Ready?" my father asked, tossing his empty bottle out the window.

CHAPTER 2

My mother had dark hair and greenish-hazel eyes, and two bathroom drawers full of makeup. The powders and creams and different-sized brushes were stacked four inches deep, and my mother could rifle around down there, one-handed without looking, and bring up the item she wanted. Our small yellow bathroom was her laboratory. Once a month she dyed her hair to get the gray out. She did it with an old rag-towel around her neck and the black ink trickling down the sides of her face while the ammonia smell must have burned a layer off her eyeballs.

A grocery store had just opened in Sebring, a bright new shiny planet with automatic double doors that slid open when you approached. My mother loved those doors. She treated it like a stage entrance, the cold air rushing up as she took off her sunglasses. Once when we walked in, a man stopped her in the aisle to say she looked like Elizabeth Taylor in *Cat on a Hot Tin Roof.*

My mother's mother was born into a family of Irish immigrants who became prosperous lawyers in Rhode Island. My grandmother's uncle was the Honorable Thomas Zanslaur

Lee, a mustachioed judge and law partner at Barney & Lee in Providence. T.Z. dined at the White House with Teddy Roosevelt and was a doting uncle to his brother's only child, a shy girl named Olive.

My grandmother Olive began speaking in a faux British accent at Miss Wheeler's, a private finishing school in Providence. Miss Wheeler believed that reading Proust was as important for a young woman as mastering a fish fork. And that's where "tomato" became "to-mah-toe" and "darling" became "dah-ling" and young Olive never made the "r" sound again.

After Miss Wheeler's, she whipped around Providence in a Stutz Bearcat with a fox stole around her neck. Her family survived the stock market crash of 1929. It wasn't the Great Depression that did in my grandmother; it was marrying a Brooklyn Irishman named Percival Desmond.

Percival and Olive: they were my maternal grandparents, though I never knew them as a married couple. They lived in a brownstone a block from Prospect Park and had three children: Percy Jr., Roderick, and the youngest, Victoria, my mother.

The 1940 US census for 483 14th Street, Brooklyn, NY, shows a big fat zero in the "income" column for Percival Desmond. My grandfather was not your classic ne'er-do-well from County Cork who drank away his paycheck. Gainful employment was his problem. He didn't care for it, despite having a law degree and a family in the coal business. He was content to live off the monthly inheritance my grandmother received from the estate of T. Z. Lee. It wasn't a lot but enough for a family of five to live on the cheap. That left my grandfather free to pursue his career as a clairvoyant. He specialized in psychometry, wherein he would hold a person's shoe or glove to his forehead and relay their future. He made the rounds of TV and radio stations in New York, where he hoped to land a regular guest appearance as a psychic.

My grandmother's time was a mystery. She took the subway into Manhattan to visit the Met or stroll along Park Avenue for hours. My mother, aged twelve, was doing the cooking and cleaning for the family. Overweight and overshadowed by her two older brothers, she was the least important presence in the apartment. She exchanged recipes with the food editor at the *Brooklyn Eagle*, baked cakes, and wrote in her diary. In a picture taken at Jones Beach, she's sitting in the sand wearing a black one-piece bathing suit, with her arm self-consciously over her stomach, next to her mugging brothers. Percy Jr. and Rod were smart, athletic, golden brown in the summer.

Until Percy Jr. got sick. My mother's diary from 1952 is one of the saddest documents I've ever read. In her twelve-year-old's loopy cursive, she recorded the deceptions wrought by adults on a terror-stricken child: a nun at Sacred Heart assured my mother that if she said her five Hail Marys and Rosaries each day Percy Jr.'s sore throat would get better. Her father told her that Percy had had a tonsillectomy. "Dad says the germ is gone," she wrote. A doctor in Boston promised successful treatments. "He said he cured every case of cancer he ever attempted. He gives us new courage. I said five Rosaries," she wrote. And then: "Percy vomits a lot. Doc says he thinks he can cure him. Please, God."

That's when my grandmother—an ethereal floater, a discusser of Monet's water lilies—made the boldest play of her life.

Acknowledging in the darkest corner of her soul that her

sixteen-year-old son might be dying, and knowing his love for fishing, my grandmother left Brooklyn in a car with three kids, suitcases, and fishing poles. Rod, only fifteen, did most of the driving, first to Florida, then Mexico, where a quack doctor in Juarez promised a miracle cancer treatment, then up the California coast to the wild surf of La Jolla, and all the way across the continent again to Florida. Percy was getting sicker and the money ran low, so they stayed there, renting a cheap apartment in St. Petersburg. The boys fished in the late afternoons at Indian Rocks Beach, catching mackerel and reds up until the last days of August.

My mother's diary entry for September 12: "Percy died. He was in a coma. It's all for the best." After that, nothing for the rest of the year, a yawning blank silence, as if she willed herself to believe that the nuns were right—"It's all for the best"—and followed her mother's lead by submerging grief as far down as possible.

They never went back to the brownstone in Prospect Park. The egg creams at Luigi's on the corner, the snatches of Yiddish arguments, the nuns at Sacred Heart—all that was in the past. My grandmother's relationship with her husband was never much to begin with. She called Brooklyn and asked him to send the rest of their belongings to St. Petersburg, then enrolled my mother and her brother at St. Paul Catholic High School. She resumed her habit of strolling for hours and riding the city buses around and around as the Florida sunlight poured through the window on her lap.

My mother did her best to distract my grandmother from her grief by achieving at school. She won debate competitions and oratory contests. She was editor of the yearbook and wrote for the student newspaper, member of the student council, president of the Spanish Club, performer of skits, recipient of scholarships.

My grandmother would say, "Oh, dahling, how marvelous," and put on a Harry Belafonte record.

NO MATTER how many accomplishments my mother racked up, she was alone with herself. When she felt lonely, she would go into the kitchen and make a lemon cake from scratch or Chinese spareribs. Food loved her back. She graduated from high school with honors, and an extra thirty pounds. Once again she turned to her diary.

"Regarding my diet I have greatly slipped and at this moment, I weigh 165 pounds, for which I am very upset. It is no one's fault but my own. I feel upset about some boy and I eat to comfort my depression. Hence, after I feel worse than before. It really is a vicious circle. I don't ask that God help me—for I should be strong enough to help myself—all I ask of Him is strength—I have so much to offer a boy, but my appearance naturally wards him off. This is my story. I resolve firmly from this moment forward to lose weight. I will!!!"

My mother's luck changed at Florida State University when she went to Mexico City on a summer study program. Judging by her scribblings on the matter, the men were dark and handsome, and didn't mind a few extra pounds. Back at school, she put herself on a punishing diet of grapefruit, milk of magnesia, cigarettes, and black coffee. Her cheekbones emerged, her stomach disappeared, and her phone began to ring.

One of the callers was a sensitive boy with Southern manners. This was my father, also a student at Florida State. They met when they both wrote for the student newspaper. He was a Kappa Sig, but he didn't fit neatly into fraternity life, except for the drinking. On Friday nights, they drove from Tallahassee to Apalachicola to eat fresh oysters the boats hauled in. My father, who had never traveled outside of Florida, found my mother sophisticated and worldly. He also sensed sadness beneath her quick humor, a sorrow he recognized in himself.

He decided it was time to bring her home to Hopewell to meet his family. My mother knew that they lived twenty miles from Tampa, a city with department stores and restaurants, and an international airport. How remote could his home be?

The day of the visit, she wore a simple black sleeveless dress and silver bangles from Mexico. The roads started getting smaller until Dad turned into the long driveway at Hopewell. "John, stop the car," Mom said, grabbing his arm in a panic. She had to take it all in: it wasn't just a house in front of her; it was a place unto its own. Towering live oaks stood over the property, dripping with so much Spanish moss they blocked off the light. Two houses were set back in deep shade. Several cars were parked out front. Dad's relatives, all who'd come to meet John's presumed fiancée.

They found her charming and funny, and they liked that she was tall, like the women at Hopewell were. They liked that John looked at her as if he'd found the one.

ONCE AS a girl I found an 8" x 10" photograph of my father taken the year he met my mother. He was handsome, wearing black square glasses, ducking his head slightly, as if he already knew he would have to take cover at some point. On the back was a long love letter written in faded green ink.

I brought it to my mother and asked what the writing said. She was making rice pudding. She kept stirring as she looked down at the picture.

"Where in the world did you find this?" my mother asked. It was typical of her to try to throw you off track.

"What does it say?" I asked, hopping around.

"It's a nice letter," she said. "Daddy is helping me make a decision."

When I took the picture to my father, he, too, read it silently to the end. He read aloud the part about dreaming of a future together. "I asked your mama to marry me," he said.

The most profound words my parents exchanged were typed or written, almost never spoken. Both were more at ease with a typewriter or a pen than their voices.

AT HOPEWELL, Big Nanny and Papa, my father's grandparents, lived in the big house. The little house was customarily reserved for the newlywed couple in the family. The idea was to help them start married life by living rent-free for a year. Big Nanny would shuffle over in the morning with freshly squeezed orange juice and a basket of warm yeast rolls. As Baptists, no one would dare call it the honeymoon suite, but enough children were conceived in that creaky wood house to busy genealogists for decades. This was the place my father brought his bride after the wedding, and ten months later I was being rocked on the porch next to the grove. My mother said she dusted me in enough Johnson & Johnson baby powder to dredge a chicken.

It's hard imagining her in the sweltering isolation of mossy Hopewell, like trying to picture Liberace living there. She taught school up until her eighth month of pregnancy. By month seven her feet were so swollen her shoes no longer fit, so she'd gone to the Salvation Army and bought a pair two sizes too big just to eke out another month before her confinement. Finally, her doctor ordered her home to rest.

My father left each morning for his job at the state employment commission office, leaving my mother to pass the hours with her feet on a hassock, pining for Peking duck and a *Life* magazine. Doing nothing drove her batty. She clipped articles from the *Plant City Courier* that she found anthropologically illuminating. NEW YORK HAS EVERYTHING—EXCEPT GRITS, PLACE TO SIT, said the headline on a feature about a local who had just visited Manhattan. But anthropology only went so far. The day before my mother's water broke that summer of 1961, the local Ku Klux Klan chapter held a rally at a roller rink a few miles down the road from Hopewell.

Underneath it all she was desperate for the happiness she was supposed to feel when starting a new life. When my father's relatives arrived with baby presents, she rushed to put on red lipstick and a roller or two in her hair to get that bounce at the bottom. She greeted the Southern Baptist well-wishers as if they'd been in Bible study together forever. After they left she lit a Marlboro. She had no idea who she was supposed to be, only that she was twenty-two, married, and a mother.

CHAPTER 3

Before I turned one, my father was offered a job with California Spray. They needed a man down at the south end of the Ridge selling pesticide to citrus growers. We left the little house at Hopewell and moved those sixty-five miles down to Sebring. Sebring was a citrus frontier where researchers came down to study the soil and new growing techniques. My mother got a job teaching fourth grade at Woodlawn Elementary School. She couldn't wait to get to work. "It's show-time," she'd say, taking her last sip of coffee before heading off to school.

Sebring was in the dead center of the state. Even if a breeze were to reach us, it would have been blocked on all sides by orange groves. The oranges were shipped north. The heat stayed put. The sun was harsher where we were, the groves less established and the land more exposed. In my childhood, Highlands County had dozens of lakes and 2.5 million citrus trees. The lakes fed the groves, which flourished in the flatwood soil. Scattered sparsely were seven thousand human inhabitants. Green botanical grids stretched out as far as the eye could see, an unstoppable army of trees, a lot of them young and newly planted. They gave the South Ridge a citrus-frontier feel, which I think my father liked—at first.

Alligators were everywhere. They lived in drainage ditches and thought nothing of crawling out of the pipes to sun themselves under your clothesline. But mosquitoes were the main plague. They bred in the nearby swamp in such quantities that the man who came to do our school pictures always brought a bottle of Calamine lotion to cover our welts. In the summer, the county mosquito truck came to our neighborhood every night at dusk. The slow, sinister way it moved up our street was hypnotic. The hissing and clanging let you know it was coming and when it rounded our corner, we stood in the grass and waited for the mechanical animal to release the marshmallow fluff of DDT. The truck passed and we fell into the mosh pit of fog, hollering because we couldn't see each other.

Every March brought the 12 Hours of Sebring endurance car race. Our Main Street was overrun with Italian drivers and Swedish models for a week. It made up for the other eleven months of quiet. You could hear the whining engines coming from the racetrack on the outskirts of town. One year I got to ride with Mario Andretti in his race car. There was a rumor that Elke Sommer made out in the Elks Club with an Italian driver. After the victory brunch, the glamor vanished as suddenly as it had appeared, and all we had was a landfill's worth of busted white Styrofoam coolers.

There was enough new stucco sparkle to make it seem like you weren't stuck in the middle of nowhere, though you really were. Our white cement block house was plunked down around other cement block houses that winked like quartz in the sun. The neighborhood was all poured concrete, hot sand, and high hopes.

It was the first house my parents owned. They splurged on a sunken living room and a corner lot. My bedroom was a monk's dorm—bed, dresser, and an electric fan. At night I knelt down on the hard terrazzo floor to say "Now I Lay Me Down to Sleep"—a mindless recitation that included the possibility that I might die before morning. My parents must have found it soothing because one or the other always stood in the doorway to listen.

My brother was across the hall. Dwight was born three years after me. When he learned to talk, he carried on long conversations with an imaginary friend named Mr. Catlick. At night the terrazzo acoustics bounced his voice off the electric fan, making it sound like Mr. Catlick really was in the room with him. Dwight had enormous feet and a thatch of blond hair that hung in front of brown eyes. He never bothered pushing it out of the way like a normal person would; he was content seeing life as a sheepdog.

Dwight was one calamity after another. If he wasn't sticking a butter knife into an electrical socket, he was turning the knobs on the gas stove. My father wrapped duct tape over the knobs, but Dwight pried it loose and torched his bangs and eyebrows. They looked like black haystacks.

All week I waited for my favorite TV show, *Get Smart*. My mother would set me up with a chicken pot pie on my own TV tray. Once, just as the *Get Smart* song started, my brother rode his tricycle into the sliding glass door and we were off to the emergency room, where he needed three stitches in his elbow.

Another time he stuck a dime in his ear. He had shoved it

in so far that only professional medical micro-tweezers could get it out. I was sick of his weekly mishaps. With the dime in his ear, I cupped my hands around my mouth and pretended to shout, pantomiming the words to make Dwight think he had gone deaf. Any normal kid would have registered terror. Dwight just looked at me with his milky little placid face and shrugged. My parents found him endearing.

In our little house in Sebring, my mother listened to Broadway musicals at a very high volume. She played her records as she cleaned the house on Saturday morning. The people in her favorite stories were always looking for the light at the end of the tunnel. Big crashing overtures followed by the loneliest solo. Also, everyone had to be singing in a foreign accent. She knew all the words and sang them, belted them out. You could be standing five feet from the vacuum cleaner shouting "MOM!" and she wouldn't hear you. My father said the music reminded her of being back in Brooklyn with the racket from the Puerto Ricans. Orange groves surrounded us, fertilizer dust was tracked in by the shoeful, but my mother was always trying to create an alternate universe inside our house.

I remember going into another kid's kitchen and his mother was sitting at a card table doing a jigsaw puzzle while her anemic transistor radio coughed out Bobbie Gentry and Glen Campbell's "Little Green Apples." After that my mother's records weren't so bad.

Woodlawn Elementary was across the road from an orange grove and a lake. Mosquitoes loved both. They swarmed in slow black clouds through the crank windows of the classrooms. The playground was a patch of sandspurs, and the teachers' parking lot was a blacktop with a few white stripes painted on it. My mother would stand in front of her fourth graders in her new J.C. Penney dress and say, "Good morning, ladies and gentlemen. Are we ready to embark?"

The fourth graders blinked back at her, with dried milk in the corners of their mouths and cowlicks rising like whirligigs from their heads. Ladies and gentlemen. They didn't think of themselves that way. At Christmastime my mother brought in a recording of "Hava Nagila" and played it, a nod to the lone Hanukkah-celebrating Jewish kid. Dancing ensued with wild klezmer spilling down the hallway.

THE PRINCIPAL had a strict dress code for his mostly female faculty. No matter the 92-degree heat, teachers had to wear stockings and heels to school every day and no pants, of course. He also had the "no wiggle rule" to tamp down on accidental undulation as the teachers walked the school hallways. Watching my mother get undressed after work in the evening was like watching Houdini squirm out of a straitjacket.

In addition to spending eight hours a day squeezed like sausages into Playtex bondage, the teachers were also wives and mothers. They were the rare group of white women in Sebring who held jobs outside of the home, and they couldn't get enough of each other.

They all belonged to the Junior Women's Club of Sebring. My mother wrote the comedy skits for their fundraisers, dragging down her typewriter from the closet and pecking out words on onion-skin paper. She spoofed small-town life but not enough to provoke a deeper examination of what their lives were becoming. To make them laugh, she would impersonate Carol Burnett doing a parody of Norma Desmond, arching her eyebrows or limping like the aged silent screen star.

My mother lived for their once-a-month shopping trips to Lakeland. They picked each other up around noon on Saturday after they finished cleaning their houses and the kids were squared away. Before leaving, my mother would pull something out of the freezer to thaw for Sunday dinner, as if a frozen chuck roast was proof that she would return. Four teachers piled into one car, two in front, two in back, passing the cigarette lighter around, laughing and smoking the whole way there.

I had glimpses of these excursions when my mother couldn't find anyone to watch me. I sat in the back seat between Barb and Marge, each hugging a hard, square purse. At school, they were Mrs. Heileg and Mrs. Jernigan. Every now and then, my mother's eyes would cut to me in the rearview mirror. "Cover your ears," she'd say.

Sometimes, they took Joan Carlton's hot car all the way to Tampa under the guise of needing to find a Cub Scout sash or fitted sheets or whatever else that couldn't be found in Sebring or Lakeland. A new shopping center had opened and they needed to see it for themselves. It was called a mall, and all the stores were under one roof, with air-conditioning.

On the drive home, the closer we got to Sebring—to husbands and children and having to start dinner that night—the quieter the car became. Marge stared out the window. Sensing the downturn, my mother reached into a shopping bag on the seat beside her and held up a new bra, dangling it in the air. That broke the silence. The other shopping bags started to rattle. One by one, each of them held up their intimates and foundations. "Cover your eyes and ears," my mother said, but they were laughing too hard to make me. Over a nightgown!

When I started at Woodlawn, my homeroom teacher was Joan Carlton. She had a swirl of brown hair like a soft-serve cone. The morning started with the Pledge of Allegiance and then everyone said in unison, "Good morning, Mrs. Carlton." It was disconcerting, seeing my mother's friend standing at a chalkboard instead of dangling a bra in the back seat of a car.

I raised my hand. "Joan, I have a question," I said.

Joan looked at me as if she'd never seen me before in her life. She kindly reminded the class that she was to be addressed as "Mrs. Carlton." Where was the wonderful giggling Joan who drank iced tea wearing shorts and flip-flops in our backyard?

THE SEVON Drive-In theater was just outside the city limits, next to an orange grove. You could see the screen jutting up out of the darkness from a quarter mile away as your car approached. My parents started taking me there the second I was old enough to be stuffed into a metal carrier that hooked over the front seat. Dwight and I wore our pajamas. That was the best part of going to the Sevon, along with setting up our encampment in the back seat. My mother passed back a roll of paper towels and the grocery bag full of buttered popcorn she made at home.

The bathroom was located near the concession stand, but the journey was too treacherous in the dark, strewn with rocks and stones, with zero visibility if the mosquito truck had just come through. Once, my mother was taking me to the bathroom and out of the white fog emerged a lady in a nightgown, holding a beer can and a fly swatter. After that, Dwight and I peed in a yellow plastic pee cup in the shape of a cowboy boot.

We watched Don Knotts in *The Ghost and Mr. Chicken*. My father loved Don Knotts, so we saw the entire canon, including the 1964 classic *The Incredible Mr. Limpet*. My mother loved Omar Sharif in *Dr. Zhivago*, but her favorite was *To Sir, with Love*, which we went to see twice. Both times, her nose-blowing woke me up. She was pressed next to my father and wiping her eyes as the Lulu song played on a hundred metal box speakers.

By the end of the evening, I was usually asleep in the back seat. Dwight was snuggled against the door with his little security blanket he called Soft N' Dry. My father would carry us to our beds when we got home. On movie nights we could pretend that everything at home was fine.

IN THE months before I got assigned as my dad's ride-along minder through the groves, a bad spring drought hit the Ridge. We went one month without rain, then two. People said it was the worst drought in fifty years.

My father sat there churning over orange groves that weren't even his. All around us, water trucks and sprinklers pumped as hard as they could. It was the same across the entire Ridge. After we ate dinner, Dad went back out to the groves to make sure the trees had gotten water that day, driving up and down the rows until it was too dark to see.

Every morning he switched on the radio on top of the refrigerator for the report from Florida Citrus Mutual. The baleful recitations of the announcers drifted down the hall to my bedroom. Misery was their specialty. They made even good news sound bad. "Tangerine futures are up," the man said, as if someone had died.

I took my bowl of Cap'n Crunch into the bathroom to watch my mother get ready for school. Her D-cup white torpedoes were pointed at the mirror. A burning cigarette hung off the edge of the counter, adding another brown tiger stripe to the Formica. Every second or third hot roller she put in her hair, she picked up the cig and took a drag. She may have been living in the dead and breezeless middle of Florida, but she didn't look it.

The room was the size of a phone booth, so I loitered half in the doorway, playing hot potato with her Clairol Kindness curlers, hemming her in. She always said this was our time together. I quizzed her on what she did at school all day and who were her favorite students and why and was it possible for her to bring me home a Little Debbie snack cake from the vending machine in the teachers' lounge. Her patience for my questions was usually endless, but lately she only half listened. Whatever starry-eyed charm she once saw in me was moving offshore, drifting farther out, and no matter how hard I swam toward it, it was a buoy I could not reach.

"Back up," she said, her voice pleading. "Give me some room."

MY MOTHER scribbled her thoughts down in a notebook she carried around in her purse. She had long conversations with the notebook. One entry she tore out, put in an envelope, and slipped into my baby book. It was an imaginary letter to me, right after she'd gone back to work after having my brother. "Oh, how Mama loves you," she told me, "and how bad I feel when I come home in the afternoon."

Cooking was her one guilt-free passion. Mothers cooked. It's what they did; only my mother wanted to cook like Joyce Chen from *Joyce Chen Cooks* on PBS. She watched the show every Saturday, taking notes on every word Joyce said on how to season a wok. Then she drove two hours to the supermarkets in Tampa to locate ingredients for Dan Dan spicy peanut sauce. She kept the procured items in their own little Joyce Chen shrine in our cabinet, doled out sparingly. She made bacon-wrapped water chestnuts twice a year—for Christmas and to take to the teachers' lounge party. I didn't appreciate sophistication being foisted on me. I wanted a mother who made pot roast.

Her cravings for egg rolls were sudden and fierce. One night when my father was gone for business, she threw Dwight and me into the car in our pajamas just to get to the closest store that sold frozen egg rolls. It was sixty miles away in Lakeland. On the way home, Dwight fell asleep with his head against the back seat door. I lay across the back seat looking up at the streaking lights of night travel, the heels of my feet propped in the window. When I awoke the next morning, I wondered if going to Lakeland to get frozen egg rolls had just been a dream. Not knowing scared me and I ran into the kitchen, relieved when I saw the empty Chun King boxes in the trash.

Another day she got home from school and said how about we go to Grant's to buy a turtle? I practically ran to the car, and the whole way to Grant's, I told her about the kid in our neighborhood who had looked right into the sun during the solar eclipse. At Grant's we didn't have to stop in the cosmetic department or look at pantyhose or pot holders. We went straight to the reptile department. Baby turtles sold for ninety-nine cents apiece. There were hundreds of them, scrabbling up the aquarium walls in desperation. They probably knew that whoever got bought would end up taped to a Hot Wheels car and left without water to die. I liked standing there next to my mother. We watched the turtles, clawing over each other to get to the top of their turtle pyramid before each one fell to the bottom.

"Pick one," my mother said, looking down at me. The intensity of her gaze was intoxicating. I couldn't decide which one. "What the hell," my mother said. "Get two."

THE DROUGHT shrunk up the lakes around us. Alligators baked on top of the sand, too parched to breed. The few who had hatchlings abandoned them to go submerge in what was left of the lake.

We lived across the street from Lake Jackson. I would sit in the yard and map out escape routes if a gator came into our front yard. If I could make it to the carport, I'd get on top of the dog food. Twenty-pound bags of Purina dog chow were stacked like sandbags, four feet high along the wall. They came from one of my father's backroads trades. He swapped grapefruit for dog food with the Purina man. My mother said she wished we could buy normal-sized boxes of things at the store. After Ortho died, we only had one dog, a skinny collie named Helene, to eat down a quarter ton of dog chow.

After Helene gave birth to five puppies, we gave four away and kept the fat one, naming him Butterball. Mother and son slept in the doghouse. One afternoon, a car slammed on its brakes in front of our house. The car stopped, but the screech of tires stayed in the air. Butterball was in the grass by the mailbox. Dad went in the house and came out with a pillowcase. Kneeling down, he stroked the puppy's soft fur as he slid the body into the pillowcase. He carried it to his car, laying it real gentle on the back seat, and drove away.

That night, my parents put an old towel down on the floor. Dad opened the back door and called Helene's name. There was just the lone jangle of one collar as she came around the corner. My father held the door open and said, "Come on, it's all right." Helene glanced at my father and then into the comforting glow of the house, then back to my father. The porch light was shining on his face. It seemed he would have stayed there all night if he had to. She came inside that night, and every night after.

She also took up a new habit of following me and my brother around outside. One afternoon we were in the backyard. The grass was dry as straw, prickly under our bare feet. Dwight had a stick in his hand, swinging it around like a sword.

"Hey, what's that?" he said. I looked to where he pointed.

The grass was moving, slowly rippling toward us. A diamondback rattler, six feet long, slithered like a sea dragon. Helene came charging out of her doghouse toward the snake, barking and baring her teeth. The snake stopped. It was shrinking in length but gathering in size.

Dwight was behind me, barefoot, shirtless, and curious. "Get back," I yelled at him. "Get up on the doghouse." I ran to the sliding glass door to call my father.

He came with his revolver. Calmly, he strode across the yard to where Helene was barking.

"Helene!" he shouted. The raw coarseness of his voice startled Helene. In the split second she swung her eyes to my father, he blasted the head off the rattlesnake. The fat rope of diamonds tightened in one last electrifying constriction before going slack. Two feet away was the head, its pink mouth and fangs open to the sky.

My insides trembled. From fear, or from the crack of the gun that still rang in my ears, I was shaking.

"Leave it alone," my father said. "Take Brother inside."

He sat down in the yard with the gun in his lap, his back to the house.

SUNDAY MORNING was devoted to the *Tampa Tribune*, the big fat newspaper that landed on our driveway wrapped in a heavy rubber band. Dad spread it out on the kitchen table while my mother made coffee. With an ashtray and the coffeepot between them, they bent over the sections as if they were back at their college paper, editing copy. The kitchen turned into a smoke-filled newsroom.

"The Brazilian juice processors are coming for us," my father said from behind the newspaper. "They're running water over citrus pulp and calling it juice."

"Huh," said my mother, who kept reading her article.

Everywhere they moved after they got married, they brought their typewriters. Now both were on the top shelf of their bedroom closet. My mother's Smith Corona was on her side above her blouses; my father's Underwood Noiseless was on his side above his shirts. Both typewriters sat quietly in the dark all day, in air that smelled of cigarette smoke and oranges. I liked going in the closet and turning on the light.

I needed to stand on a chair to reach the string and yank it down, and right before the light bulb popped on, there were the two typewriters looking at each other in the dark. In high school my father imagined himself as the next Mickey Spillane, writing crime fiction. So far he had only written an article about pesticides for an agricultural trade paper.

THE *TAMPA Tribune* was 250 pages on Sundays and my father read almost every word of it. He read about the proposed tax hike, he read about the trash burn, he read about the Jaycees leadership changes, and he read about the Viet Cong and the ladies' society news column called "Where Are You Going? Quo Vadis?" When it seemed he was finished, he flipped to the crossword and folded the newspaper into a tight square so that only the puzzle showed.

My mother went off to get ready, even though there was nothing to get ready for. The stores were closed. The library was closed. The streets were empty. It gave my mother such a trapped feeling that sometimes she got in her car and drove to the only place that was open—the gas station—and bought a roll of Certs, just to buy something.

"What's a three-letter word for an Arab hat with a tassel?" my father called out. My mother stuck her head out of the bathroom with a mascara wand in her hand. "Fez?"

I got saddled with Dwight every Sunday morning. We weren't allowed to go outside or even sit in the carport until noon because my parents thought kids playing in the yard on Sunday morning was an advertisement for paganism. Maybe my father could hear Big Nanny's disapproval at the idea of skipping church or my mother couldn't escape the evil voice of Sister Clarice. Neither was comfortable with flaunting our non-churchgoing ways to the neighborhood. The one Sunday of the year we went was on Easter, to an Episcopalian church. It was like getting dressed up to go to a play.

As the morning dragged on, I heard the sound of car doors slamming and ran to the window. "The Stanleys are home from church," I yelled, to no effect. The clock on the stove refused to advance.

At the stroke of noon, I would run for daylight, tearing outside with a bologna sandwich and my telescope. The Cap'n Crunch people had billed it as a spy telescope. The "glass" was plastic and the magnifying power to see things had been overstated, but I carried it everywhere to let others know they may be subject to monitoring.

My parents seemed restless after they finished the newspaper. My mother decided to alphabetize the spice rack. My father, shaved and dressed, announced that he should probably go check on the sprinklers in a grove. Dwight looked up, in the hopes he'd be asked to ride along. "Not this time, Son," Dad said, putting his hand on top of my brother's head. I couldn't see my mother's face behind the cabinet, but the spice jars stopped clinking and went silent.

AFTER TWELVE weeks without rain, the deluge came in June. The headline on my sixth birthday, June 8, 1967, took up half the front page: RAINS DRENCH COUNTY TO END FOUR MONTHS DRY SPELL. STATE WAS DRIEST IN 25 YEARS.

The citrus groves in Central Florida perked back to life. The world was a different place—quenched, swollen, sprouting, and phosphorous green. The muscle in my father's neck stopped jumping under his skin. But the rain didn't let up. It kept raining. The wet conditions brought on the possibility of fungal root rot, giving my father a new reason to doodle hangmen.

Some evenings, Mom would take me on an ice cream run. There was a drive-through convenience mart not far from us called Farm Stores. We waited our turn to reach the sliding glass door where the lady stuck her head out for our order. An electric bug zapper hung from the ceiling in the carport. It was the size of a space heater, and every few seconds a flying insect exploded in a violent flash of light, like a stun grenade, right over the dairy case. I was in the passenger seat in my pajamas. The night air was so humid that my mother rolled through a couple stop signs to make it home before the ice cream turned to soup.

My father went to Farm Stores alone. He drove the slow loop of Sebring, flinging the empties of a six-pack of beer from his window—into ditches, orange groves, and out near the racetrack.

CHAPTER 4

The closest thing to glamor Sebring had was a forty-two-year-old citrus baron named Von Maxcy who lived out on Sparta Road. One night, Von Maxcy came home from work and someone threw a pillowcase over his head. He was stabbed multiple times and shot in the head. His wife found his body on the purple shag carpet in their bedroom. I was in kindergarten when it happened, but the drama gripped the town for the next two years.

The Maxcy family was citrus and cattle royalty in Central Florida. Von Maxcy's ranch in Sebring was big enough for him to land his plane on his own airstrip behind his swimming pool. His house had an entertainment room with a platform for a go-go dancer. Whenever we were outside playing and heard a propeller in the sky, we stopped whatever game we had going and searched the clouds for Von Maxcy's twin-engine. The first one to spot his plane would shout, "There goes Von Maxcy."

After divorcing his first wife, Von Maxcy laid eyes on a dark-haired fruit sorter named Irene who worked in his family's packing house. Irene had black hair, pointy boobs, and a country face. "Shapely" is the word people used to describe Irene, who signed her name with an *X* at the beauty parlor and had the bills sent to Von Maxcy.

After the murder, my father went around the house at night rattling the doors to make sure they were locked. My mother stopped watching *Alfred Hitchcock Presents* in her nightgown in front of the sliding glass door. Our old girl Helene was not a guard dog; she was a brittle-boned septuagenarian in a silky fur coat. Still, my father petted her with new respect. He said a dog is the best protection you can have. He also had another gun in the closet, inside a Florsheim shoe box on the top shelf next to his typewriter. I wasn't supposed to tell Dwight.

Dad knew Von Maxcy's uncle, Latt Maxcy, the head of the Maxcy business empire, who lived a half-hour drive away in Frostproof. Dad went back and forth over whether he should pay him a sympathy call. He got out his shoeshine kit and used the soft brush on his brogans, debating it with my mother as she put on her makeup. He felt a simple handshake at a funeral was not enough. He wanted to acknowledge to the old man that an empire had been shaken. Dad said he would call his friend George LaMartin to see if he was going to the funeral. My mother said he was overthinking it.

News reporters poured into town to cover the story. A flock of them took over the lunch counter at Gilbert Drugs, and one day Dad and I went to look at them. Sports coats and camera bags were strewn everywhere, so nobody else had room to sit. They spoke in loud voices and did not say "thank you" when the waitress topped off their coffee. One guy put his cigarette out in his grilled cheese! They seemed focused on something so important that nothing else mattered.

Dad and I were down at the far end of the counter waiting for a seat when the men suddenly jumped up, grabbed their things, and ran out of Gilbert's. A waitress who began cleaning up their mess casually told us the police chief had probably called a press conference. I felt bad for Von Maxcy getting killed and all, but his murder made life exciting, especially when the trial started.

First it came out Irene had been having an affair with a Yankee she met at the Elks Club. Then it came out the two were behind the murder. Women criminals didn't come along every day; in that regard, Irene Maxcy was a trailblazer.

I got my Irene Maxcy news from Ceola, who came to our house five days a week. She had tobacco skin and broad cheekbones, and she wore a glossy black wig like the Supremes. Her real name was Theora, but because of her broad cheekbones and a few drops of Indian blood, people called her Ceola, after Osceola, the legendary leader of the Florida Seminoles. Only my father addressed her by her given name.

Ceola was an avid follower of crime and misdeeds committed by Sebring's elite. She got her information from the newspaper, but the really good stuff came from friends who passed things along from their observation posts in restaurant kitchens, caddy shacks, and shoeshine stands. Both accounts had their own biases and blind spots. Taken together, minus the bald-faced lies, Ceola probably knew more about the Maxcy case than all the investigators put together.

MY PARENTS paid Ceola five dollars a day to watch Dwight and me, in addition to light housework. She wore a white polyester uniform and kept a pack of Kools in her front pocket and preferred fishing to ironing, which is how I came to know every lake in Sebring. My mother told Ceola many times that the uniform wasn't necessary, until finally my father said, "Vicki, quit hounding her. She is comfortable the way she is."

My mother's fumbling approach as a liberal Yankee made her an outsider to my father's relationship with Ceola. When Ceola's car was broken, it was my father who ferried her home. The Seaboard and Atlantic Coast Line train tracks divided white Sebring from Black Sebring. Her side of the tracks had many names. Boot Town, Colored Town, Coon Town, or the Quarters. The proper name was Washington Heights, but I never heard anyone use it.

Ceola's part of Sebring felt like a separate town. Time slowed and the heat was worse. Ceola and her husband, Clarence, lived in a tiny turquoise house with no telephone. It was on the corner, across from an orange grove and the town dump. Chickens roamed the streets. When Clarence, who drove a tractor in the groves, was needed in the fields, he would be summoned by word of mouth; from the groves across the tracks to Ceola's house and right to Clarence.

My brother and Ceola had a rocky start. Her white shoes moved silently from tub to toilet, stepping around my brother, who watched her from his baby bouncer like a one-year-old prince in pajama bottoms. He stared at her silver cat-eye glasses while he sucked his bottle. A few weeks into her tenure, she was at the kitchen sink with Dwight on her hip as she warmed a jar of baby food under hot water. He grabbed her nose and then her ear. Ceola told him to quit it, but he kept on, grabbing a fistful of her hair until his hand came away with a black wig. He wailed in shock as Ceola put him down, picked her wig up off the linoleum, and calmly put it back on her short braids.

My brother kept his distance after that.

I belonged with Ceola more than anywhere else. I clung to her fiercely. She called me Shadow, exhaling air from her cheeks as if she were stuck with me.

Each morning she arrived exactly five minutes before the start of *Captain Kangaroo*, and in some mystical transition of power, my mother vanished, and it seemed as if Ceola had been there for a thousand years. I would have stayed home with her for the rest of my life.

We had our routines. The vacuum started after *Captain Kangaroo* was over. We ate our lunch at 11:30 and then watched *Guiding Light* while we folded laundry and *Another World* if there was ironing. In the afternoon, Ceola opened her black pocketbook and brought out two sticks of Wrigley's Juicy Fruit gum, one for her and one for me, and we popped our gum on our back teeth until Dwight woke from his nap.

Throughout the day, Ceola sprayed us with OFF! We used it in the carport so the poison wouldn't drift onto the living room furniture. Close your eyes, she said, spraying my head. I asked her what she did when the mosquito truck came through in the evening belching marshmallow fog. She said the truck didn't come down her street. "How come?" I asked. The county truck didn't come across the tracks, she said.

The next time the mosquito truck came down our street, I flashed on Ceola and Clarence sitting on their front porch being swarmed by mosquitoes. I jumped into the fog with the other kids, but it was no fun after that.

CEOLA LOVED to fish. The lakes started to call for her around three in the afternoon, at which time she'd leave a note on the counter for my parents saying that the children pestered her into taking them fishing. We'd stop first at her house to pick up her cane poles and bait. In her backyard, she had a large covered wooden bin. Inside was the blackest soil I'd ever seen. It smelled like manure and old dinner scraps that had baked in 95-degree heat for a month. And it was full of worms, fat and pink, that Ceola raised expressly for fishing. Anyone who fished wanted some of that bait. She tied the cane fishing poles to the side of her car and we headed for the shore of Lake Sebring, where we sat on overturned bait buckets with long poles in our hands.

One afternoon it was me and Ceola and a bunch of men headed to a different lake, where I'd never been. Hardly anyone talked after we left the car. A man in a straw hat led the way. The rest of us followed, walking single file carrying cane poles. Weeds slashed like buggy whips at my bare legs. There was no sandy shore to speak of and no dock and not a single swimmer. We trudged along until we came to a drainage pipe. The opening was at least five feet around, an alligator motel if there ever was one, but this contingent didn't think twice about setting up there. Soon I saw why. Within ten feet of the drainpipe, the water was churning with fish.

The man with the bread sack hanging from his belt loop glared at Ceola, then at me. He didn't appreciate Ceola bringing a white child to their lake. He untied the plastic bag and pulled out a piece of bread. As he baited his hook, he spit, then he gathered his things and moved farther down the bank of the lake, away from us. Ceola threw her line out and watched her bobber.

Lakes were everywhere in Sebring, dozens of them. They weren't officially segregated; everybody just knew which lake was theirs. I went swimming at Dinner Lake and Lake Jackson, which had a pine-shaded trail that led from the road down to the water. The dock had the perfect length of runway for a heaving leap. It was high enough that you had time to figure out midair what you wanted to do. The second your toes left the wood you were higher than everyone else on the dock, and their screams of "Cannonball!" or "Jackknife!" sounded like faint music on some far-off radio. A girl in Polk County misjudged the depth of the water after a drought and hit headfirst on the lake bottom. She was in an iron lung, but for a few seconds she had been airborne like me.

WHEN I came in the house, Ceola would fix me a sandwich. She used two flimsy pieces of white bread as a cargo hold for a half-cup of mayonnaise. She added a thick slice of Ruskin tomato and set the sagging paper plate on the table, then sat across from me reading the newspaper. Von Maxcy's murder trial was about to start, his wife charged with the crime. Irene Maxcy's black eyes burned a hole through the front page of the paper, which obscured Ceola's face.

"Mm, mm, mm," Ceola said, taking in new information that she hadn't known.

"What does it say?" I demanded. She continued to ignore me.

"It's our paper," I said.

The newspaper lowered down. Her face was without expression, a blank stone with blank eyes. It probably wasn't the first time a child in her care had asserted employer privilege, but it was the first time I had.

My legs began to swing on their own accord under the table. I wanted her to send me to my room, to get away from the way she looked at me. Instead, she returned to her reading and ignored me with fresh intensity.

"Lord have mercy," Ceola said at last. "She's fixing to go to the electric chair."

I knew about the electric chair. You sat in it and died, and it was very heavy and faraway, at least it had been until I imagined Irene Maxcy and her milky white arms being strapped to the wood. Getting to know Irene all these months from the newspaper made her a real person. She shopped at the same grocery store we did. Even the possibility that Irene Maxcy might be sent to the electric chair meant it was possible for any lady at Publix to be sent there. And if Irene Maxcy went to the chair, part of us went with her, too.

Ceola never shared another word about the case. She said quit asking her and there'd be trouble if I pestered her. She didn't read the newspaper anymore. It sat on the table between us, dead.

INSTEAD OF taking the summer off like most teachers, my mother took classes at a college in Lakeland. Then it was time to go back to her classroom to get ready for the new school year. One of those late August days she called Ceola from school to say she had forgotten a key she needed. "Lord have mercy," Ceola said, after she hung up the phone. Translation: "I don't have time for this foolishness."

We drove the key up to school. First, we went to the principal's office, where the secretary tried to raise my mother on the intercom in her classroom. "Vicki?" she said. "Vicki, are you there?" Not "Mrs. Hull?" The familiarity and coziness came as a shock.

Check the teachers' lounge, the secretary suggested. We walked down the empty hall, freshly waxed to a welcoming gloss. Ceola carried her black pocketbook. At the door marked "Teachers' Lounge," Ceola knocked. We could both hear noise on the other side. Ceola knocked again.

I had always thought of the teachers' lounge as a dour hideaway with a table where the teachers could eat their sandwiches or perhaps use the phone. If my mother had to call home during the day, it was always from the teachers' lounge. The phone number was written on the inside wood of our kitchen cabinet. I associated it with emergency, necessity, and hushed conversations.

Someone finally heard the knocking. It wasn't so much a person that greeted us as a back draft of cigarette smoke and possibly the sound of a jazz trumpet. There was laughter, paper plates everywhere, a real roaring party. None of the teachers wore dresses. They were in pants or dungarees, their hair loosely pulled back. I saw my mother. A crowd was gathered around her, laughing uproariously as she did her Gloria Swanson imitation. Her entire being was electrified in performance, until she noticed Ceola and me. The sight of us drained the voltage from her body. Ceola rummaged in her pocketbook for the key.

CHAPTER 5

I was nut-brown and streaked blond and wearing color-coordinated clothes my mother bought on her solitary trips to the mall. On the summer days I wasn't driving with Dad, I would leave the house with a shirt on, but I'd pull it off and run free with the neighborhood boys.

Not far from our home was Highlands Hammock State Park, a spooky nine-thousand-acre cypress swamp crawling with alligators. An old-timey sign from the 1940s was posted near the entrance with a word of warning about the gators:

> A MESSAGE FROM OUR WILDLIFE.
> PLEASE, PLEASE. DON'T FEED ME.
> I'M NOT TAME, BUT WILD, YOU SEE.
> WHILE I DO NOT INTEND TO HARM,
> I MIGHT TAKE OFF AN ARM.

A narrow boardwalk stretched across the top of the dark bayou. Panthers and bears came near when the water table was low, but mostly the park was a humid, stinking wetlands of reptiles and amphibians croaking from the muck. After a rain, the fish were always biting.

We weren't regulars at Highlands Hammock because the bird people usually clogged the boardwalks with their sober note-taking. But the recent rains after the drought had shut the place down, making the entire swamp ours.

"Wait for me," Dwight called, following my friend Scotty and me into the park one afternoon. Scotty lived down the street in a white stucco house that sparkled in the sunshine. He rode a green ten-speed and was missing part of his right hand from a Fourth of July mishap with an M80. He could still fish and shoot BB guns and do all kinds of normal stuff except hold a pencil in school. He was in the process of training himself to be left-handed.

Usually we occupied ourselves by retrieving golf balls from the pond at the golf course by our houses. The pro shop paid us a dime for each ball we brought back. The water hazards were mud traps where gators lounged, so one of us dove for the golf balls while the other kept watch. We had to dive fast.

At the cypress swamp, a single rotten guardrail separated us from the water. Scotty set up his spot to fish, untying his bag of hot dog buns. We rolled the soft bread into little white balls and baited our hooks. Down in the water, the garfish looked like they were playing bumper cars. Within a few minutes, a fish belly flopped where Scotty lowered his line and I crouched down beside him.

"Got one!" he said. The puny splash was followed by a much bigger splash in the distance. We looked up, but there was only the empty boardwalk that disappeared into the dark swamp. We scrambled to our feet and ran toward the sound.

It was Dwight, chest-high in the inkwell trying to climb out of the water. He wasn't crying or hollering or anything, but the wood was too slimy with algae and he kept sliding down it like it was a firepole.

"Thanks for ruining everything," I told him.

Scotty used his good hand to hold on to the railing and he stretched his Fourth of July hand down toward the water. It looked smaller and more flipper-like over the black water.

"Grab hold!" Scotty said.

Gators move quietly, with a stillness before destruction. Scotty was the first to spot the bull gator turning in the dark water. The gator rotated in a slow circular sweep until he faced my brother.

"Pull!" I shouted, my wet skin next to Scotty's on the boardwalk. A superhuman strength came over Scotty.

Dwight latched on to our outstretched arms and we dragged him onto the boardwalk, scraping the skin off his chest as our screams echoed over the silent swamp.

We landed Dwight. The bull gator blinked and floated away.

SCOTTY WAS the most fleet-footed creature on the block; no shirt, no shoes, just a pair of ragged cutoffs that let him fly from yard to yard, with feet as tough as cowhide. His chest was runty and his hair shorn to the nub, POW-style, compliments of his grandmother's backyard barbershop. That's how all the boys I knew got their haircuts—taken out in the backyard and buzzed like a dog.

Scotty lived with his grandparents. His real parents had sent him to Florida like a package and never picked him up. The old folks made it up to him with boxes of sugary cereal, which helped us amass our spy paraphernalia.

Between the two of us, we had every spy gadget the cereal companies had to offer—the Quisp Cosmiclouder Gun, the Cap'n Crunch Bo'Sun whistle, the Chex Secret Agent Decoder Ring, plus maps and telescopes we used for surveillance on neighbors. We sat in the Bermuda grass and made a pair of walkie-talkies with twenty feet of string. Scotty's grandma had washed the tin cans, but they still smelled like fruit cocktail.

Scotty gave me a can, took the other one, backed up to make the long string taut, and told me to interrogate him.

"What are you doing right now?" I said into my can. His shirtless chest caved with disappointment.

"Ask a real question," he said. That was Scotty. He didn't let you slide.

A Frankenstein-shaped shadow fell across the grass. It was the neighborhood sadist, Conrad Jenkins, a brawny-shouldered menace who burned holes in lizards with a magnifying glass. The previous Fourth of July, while we were lighting smoke bombs and sparklers, he shot a bottle rocket at the rabbit cage in my backyard. The poor rabbits shit a thousand pellets when the missile hit. Conrad claimed it was an accident, but everyone knew he would have used a stick of dynamite if he had one.

"You two playing with dolls?" he said to Scotty, ignoring the walkie-talkies in our hand.

We dropped our cans and followed him to another kid's house, where two boys were panting in the grass. We drank out of the backyard hose and flopped down. Conrad insisted we pretend Sebring Shores was under attack by Japanese kamikaze pilots. A frothy white foam had started to collect in the corners of his mouth. He shouted in a red-faced rage, "Incoming!" We were supposed to pick up our pretend machine guns and shoot down the kamikazes while running for cover. The stick felt too much like a stick to be a machine gun, so I tossed it down, infuriating Conrad. "Kill Them Japs!" he ordered, waiting for me to pick up the stick.

I glanced at Scotty, who had receded into the trio of boys. He watched with detachment as Conrad asked me again if I was a Jap lover. I hated that kid. It was now or never.

"It's Vietnam now, you dunce!" I yelled and hauled ass to the safety of my carport. Conrad broke out into a full sprint. I just had to reach my property before he did, and then I could stop him cold with the magic words: "I'll charge you with trespassing!" It was our understanding of the law that we could file criminal charges if someone came onto our property without permission. But we were law-abiding citizens afraid of being taken away in handcuffs, and Conrad was not.

Swatting aside the trespassing charge, he burst into the yard holding a piece of wood he'd torn off a fence.

"Nice knowing ya," one of the onlookers yelled. I stood alone in the grass as Conrad closed in with the plank in his hand.

I heard commotion behind me, and suddenly Helene, our gentle elderly collie, shot past in a blur of satanic snarling and white incisors. Conrad froze, eyes closed, too terrified to move. We couldn't believe what we were seeing. Conrad was afraid of dogs. Helene stood her ground, fur bristled, growling low in her throat as Conrad edged away.

My friendship with Scotty never recovered. I went around telling everyone he played with dolls.

THE NEW phone book for Highlands County had so many new names and businesses that it seemed like we lived in a different place. The thickness wafted a fresh smell. Suddenly, the old phone book seemed like an inaccurate reflection of our community's vibrancy. I took ours from the trash and made it my own phone book. I studied the names in the white pages. Lone female names were likely spinsters and widows who weren't out doing things. I tried them first. One lady said a phone was not a toy and I should not be treating it as such; otherwise I would have asked if her refrigerator was running. A lady named Varnadoe stayed on the line for a while. She said she had gout. She told me all about it, on that and other calls. She seemed to enjoy the company, but then I started worrying that she was trying to keep me on the line so the police could trace the call. One day she asked, "Honey, are you lonely?" I said no and scratched her off my call list.

ONE SUNDAY, the Funny Face drink company ran a quarter-page ad in the comic section. "Are you over the age of four and not yet in business for yourself?" Funny Face had just launched a new national contest. The entry form was in the ad. All you had to do was state in writing why Funny Face was better than Kool-Aid. The boy winners would be awarded a red-and-white-striped vinyl tent with a steel tube frame. The girls got a doll collection. To hell with that. I wanted a tent. I mailed in my entry form accordingly.

Six weeks later, the tent arrived in a box addressed to Andrew Hull.

The red-and-white-striped tent was a lot smaller in real life, and made of plastic, but it could accommodate two people. All the boys in the neighborhood came over to look at it;

I wanted Jessie to come over to see it. Jessie was our twelve-year-old babysitter. Whenever she babysat us, she brought her baton and practiced in the driveway until it got dark and time for our bath. At the school competition, she wore a fake hair bun, but babysitting she wore her hair loose, which I thought looked better that way. Her forehead had acne. No one else had acne. She could throw that baton sky-high.

I understood why boys played army, because there was a distinct possibility they might one day be soldiers. A baton? What could you do with that? But if anyone could make it in baton, Jessie could.

After my father set up the tent, I asked Jessie if she wanted to try it out, and she accepted. We both lay down in the humid plastic stink of the brand-new tent. We stayed until the mosquitoes drove us home.

THE WEEK before I started first grade my mother took me to Whataburger for a milkshake. As we sat in the car waiting for our milkshakes, she announced it was no longer acceptable for me to go shirtless in public.

It didn't come out that smooth. She'd start a sentence and then stop, thinking of a better way to phrase something. Her nervousness made me nervous. It was as if she'd raked through her *Psychology Today* magazine for guidance, all for a cotton shirt. The shirt topic had come up before, but she never enforced it. Now she was talking about the seasons of life and the wonderfulness of girlhood, none of which she sounded a hundred percent sold on herself.

I'll tell you what made me sad: the apology in her voice

that signaled that the Whataburger shirt eulogy marked the official kickoff of all the eulogies to come. The waitress showed up with our milkshakes. I never left the house again without a shirt. At least I got a milkshake out of it.

CHAPTER 6

I was named after my father's sister, my aunt Anne, a nervous auburn beauty who liked to look at sewing patterns and smoke. Everything she owned snapped shut—her cigarette pouch, her lipstick case, her white suitcase. When she came to visit, the entire weekend was a series of clicks. She and Ceola had the same purse with a hard clasp that had a little gold thing on top. If she got thirsty, she'd touch her throat like a sick patient and say to me, "Honey, would you mind getting me a Co'Cola?"

My mother was always reminding me what an honor it was to be named after Aunt Anne. I saw it as a curse.

I was the antithesis of everything she stood for. Grub in my fingernails, ashy knees, and knotted hair that smelled like lake water: her eyes traveled over me, pausing at each transgression. She took a keen interest in my "presentation." She said "presentation" is a girl's chance to make a good impression on the world. Once she bought me a little cuticle kit.

Every visit, she'd snap open her suitcase, pull out a box, and shake it at me.

"Guess!" she'd say.

It was never a camping kit. It was always a doll. She kept hoping the right one would crack open the vault of my disinterest. I'd been trained to say thank you. "Oh, you are so welcome, honey," she said.

Her gifts made me feel bad about myself but also made me mad; she willfully ignored who I was. My mother's approach was not as severe. Not yet, anyway.

I didn't see how anyone could marry Aunt Anne, but someone did, and he was the most interesting, funny man in the world. His name was Burt. He and Aunt Anne lived in Boynton Beach and drove over to see us every three or four months. When Burt got out of the car, he came at me like a lowland gorilla and swept me up in the air with his furry forearms that smelled of Hai Karate cologne. He was a salesman, traveling around the state with his clothes swinging on a pole across his back seat. Burt didn't have the slightest reverence for oranges. He looked at my father as if he were crazy to worry so much. "Jesus Chrysler, John, it's 1967 and there are easier ways to make a living," he told Dad.

When Burt's car was parked in our driveway, I liked to sit in the back seat with the shirts and imagine that I was traveling alone, eating in motel coffee shops and using ice buckets.

When Burt came out to the car for Aunt Anne's carton of cigarettes, I asked him to tell me the story. What story, he said, playing dumb. The story, I said, when you found me.

When I was three, I got out of bed and somehow slipped past Burt and Aunt Anne and my parents as they played cards at the dining room table. I must have been sleepwalking, and very stealthily, because I got out the front door unnoticed. I crossed the yard, crossed the darkened road, and went down to the lake, where after a frantic search, Burt found me sitting at water's edge, soaking wet and content beneath the moon. Once my mother's hysteria subsided and a new lock was put on our front door and the fright of the incident faded, Burt put me in one of his stories, saying I was this close to being a midnight snack for a ten-foot alligator.

Aunt Anne and Burt came for a visit that fall. There was something odd about it. My mother made her signature bacon-wrapped water chestnuts and it wasn't even Christmas. Burt must have eaten ten of them while he and Dad sat in the living room talking. He was the kind of person who said whatever came to his mind, without regard for fact or experience, and this entertained my father, who was fact-based and sincere. Burt looked at my father and said very solemnly, "For the next forty-eight hours I don't want to hear a goddamn word about oranges."

"Burt, please," Aunt Anne said.

Dad claimed that all the boys were in love with Aunt Anne in high school. On weekends she worked in the box office of the movie theater, and boys would line up just to buy a ticket from her. This was hard to imagine.

The one thing that no one ever mentioned about Aunt Anne was her deformed thumb. It looked like a hammerhead shark, smooth and slab-like, and nothing you'd want on you. My stomach did a flip if it brushed against me.

THE REASON for Aunt Anne and Burt's visit in the fall was never stated, but Aunt Anne spent a lot of time telling my father that she was concerned he was running himself into the ground. She commented on the dark circles under his eyes, the gray crescents that ran on their side of the family. "John, you are going to work yourself to death if you're not careful, just like Daddy," she said.

It made me uneasy when I saw the two of them together, how similar they were. Their cigarettes burned down in their fingertips as they contemplated the fragility of one situation or another. Aunt Anne was older by three years, but being deeply Southern, she deferred to my father, who also being deeply Southern, deferred to his elder sister.

In the afternoon my father went to two different package stores to track down Burt's favorite Scotch, Cutty Sark, with a picture of a clipper ship on the label. The next morning Burt and Aunt Anne were bright-eyed and eating toast at the table. My mother was in the kitchen alone. Dad didn't appear for hours. Mom held the empty Cutty Sark bottle up to the window, turning it slowly in the light.

It was the last time I saw Burt. He and Aunt Anne got a divorce. After the split, she was too fragile to continue her campaign with me. She still looked at sewing magazines and all her accouterments snapped shut with an annoying click, but her faith in the power of presentation was shaken.

CHAPTER 7

After Aunt Anne's visit, my grandmother Gigi showed up. She was due at our house Friday by 4 p.m. for a weekend visit. My father kept checking his watch and going outside to see if her car was coming down the road.

"I told Mama, 'Mama, I will come get you and carry you home on Sunday,'" he said, cracking some ice at the sink. He loved his mother, but she also irritated him.

The timing of Gigi's visit was also strange. It wasn't my birthday or Dwight's birthday, which is when she usually visited us in Sebring. She also didn't usually drive. She would make the seventy-five-mile trip from Plant City on a Greyhound. That must have been interesting because the bus stopped in several one-stoplight towns. I could picture Gigi in her Jackie Kennedy pillbox hat wrestling her bag of peanuts loose from a gas station vending machine while the entire bus waited.

At our birthday parties, she was the only adult to wear a birthday hat. The elastic rubber string would cut into her soft fleshy neck and her smile was vacant, as if she were time traveling. I didn't know her very well, but I liked that she wore a birthday hat. What I didn't like was that she was the mother of Aunt Anne. The mother of someone who reapplied lipstick between Cokes was bound to enforce the code of femininity twice as hard. I would have to be on guard all weekend.

Gigi came from a good family in Plant City, where her father was a prominent banker. They were Methodists, which in Plant City was the more progressive wing of conservatism. When Gigi was younger, she was a boldface name in the society pages. Her life was a whirlwind of bridal teas and engagement luncheons at the Plant City Country Club, where they played canasta and ate lemon chiffon cake. She was an outlier in the family she married into, a trained pianist who had little interest in country life at Hopewell.

My father's father was the rapscallion of his family, sent to a military academy in Georgia after slugging his high school principal. How and where he met Gigi I do not know, because my father never talked about him, as if it were best to leave some things unspoken. I know he was a fruit buyer and a whiz with figures, able to compute crop yields and profit margins lightning fast in his head. He would also stop at a bar in the middle of the day on his way home from the weekly vegetable and fruit auction.

He was famous for his marksmanship. At Hopewell, he could shoot an orange clean off the branch with his Walther P38. He drank himself to death at forty-six, when my father was a senior in high school. Later on, I heard stories about the old man's propensity to point the gun at his family when he was drunk. One night, or so one story goes, he lined them up in the front yard and took aim like an executioner, all of them—Gigi, my dad, and my aunt Anne. He terrorized them until the sheriff's deputy rolled up. Then it turned to humil-iation, Gigi standing in the damp grass of her front yard in a nightgown with her children as the deputy told my father's father to go on inside and sleep it off.

When Gigi finally pulled into our driveway in her bat-winged car, she looked like an arriving medic with her small white suitcase. My mother had rushed home earlier to make Gigi's favorite artichoke dip. It looked like wet papier-mâché baked in a casserole dish. Gigi clasped her hands and said, "Oh Vicki, you know how I love *artichaut*." Gigi knew about twenty French words and drummed up any reason to use them.

She doted on my father as if he were helpless, fixing his tea the way he liked it and telling him everything would be fine and that he had simply exhausted himself. They filled up ashtray after ashtray and emptied multiple bowls of sugar into their pitchers of iced tea.

After one of her buck-up sessions with my father, Gigi came into my bedroom to lie down. She tidied her things, rearranging her perfume and her brush and mirror set, care-ful not to disturb the warhorses I had galloping on my dresser in a fierce V-formation. She set up her own V-flank with her toiletries. You could tell which one was her favorite because she moved it an inch forward from the others. Her big bot-tle of Shalimar took the spotlight. She was just finishing the alignments and turning away from the dresser when she bent over to look closer at the warhorses. One of her butterfly hands swooped in and picked up an Appaloosa, its nostrils flaring. She studied it with grave interest. I stood there not breathing and watching.

She returned the Appaloosa to the herd. She must have figured we had bigger problems than my toy preference at the moment. She lowered herself onto the bed with a weight-less grace.

"Come talk to Gigi," she said, patting the place beside her. She was a torrent of news. She said her ladies from the United Daughters of the Confederacy were going with red poinsettias again for the annual cotillion. Oh, and the loveliest man had come over to tune the piano, and do you know what he said? He said it wasn't every day he got to tune a white piano. Gigi said this tickled her so much that she sat right down for the man and played "Greensleeves." She spoke in a breathy Southern drawl, with the airflow squeezing up through too-small windpipes and forced out with charm. It sounded like she'd been socked in the breadbasket with the butt of a Yankee rifle. A Brach's peppermint was clicking around on one of her back molars. It was hard not to be mesmerized.

Finally, she got down to business. "About your daddy," she said, folding her hands in her lap. "He has been under a great deal of pressure. He just needs some wind put back in his sails."

Vague bromides were the stock-in-trade of my father's family, but this one got my attention. "What kind of wind?"

Gigi was not profound or even strong-willed; any brave impulse would have been tamped down by all the Valium and Librium she took. Her doctor wrote prescriptions with a free hand, trapping her in amber. That weekend I had seen her in a chair with a book when the ash on her Tareyton broke off and crashed into her lap like the Hindenburg, the fiery embers startling her awake. But sitting in my bedroom, she emerged from the fog and spoke the truth.

"The wind that lets a person sail," she said, smiling.

On Sunday, I put her white suitcase in the trunk of the car as she started the engine. She waved. "Bye, honey!"

"Bye, Gigi," I yelled, sprawled in the grass.

A week later a present came in the mail. Wrapped in tissue was a unicorn.

CHAPTER 8

The Frost Warning Service put out an urgent bulletin on February 8, 1968, that a cold front was pushing down from the north. It was the middle of first grade. My father had been up before dawn listening to the radio. The aluminum windows in our house were defenseless against the cold, but our warmth was beside the point. It was the oranges that had to be kept warm. They were predicting a hard freeze, which meant the fruit would be exposed to below-freezing temperatures for an extended period of time. If a hard freeze were to linger for two or three nights, millions of boxes of oranges would be lost.

My father set out in the cold February sunlight to find Booker; they needed to raise a crew of men to spend the night in the groves, keeping the trees warm. Some nights my father took me along. I stayed bundled up in the back seat of his Ford, watching the men lighting the fires around the trees, their single-minded dedication to warmth nearly a maternal act. The men shivered in the cold, their breaths brittle holograms in the darkness. I would fall asleep to the sounds of their voices and then awaken as the car door opened. It was my father reaching into the glove box for a bottle. He'd run me home before midnight and return to spend the rest of the night in the groves tending the fire with the crew. That February freeze, crisis was averted. The trees stayed warm enough to survive the cold string of nights.

BUT TWO months later in April, with Valencia season underway, something bad happened on the TV. When I came home from school, Ceola wasn't there as she usually was. Our babysitter from down the street, Jessie the majorette, was there. Mom came home from work and turned on the TV in the living room. A man had been shot. It was the man on Ceola's church fan, Dr. Martin Luther King. The fan was on the wall in her guest room along with another fan. One man was dead and soon the other would be, too.

That night my parents sat outside on rotting patio furniture. The air was cool. The orange blossoms were finished and dropping from the trees. My father told my mother how he'd gone looking for Booker first thing that morning. He found him in one of the groves, where his crew was pulling in Valencias. Dad didn't know quite what to say or if Booker should speak first, but said he figured he'd better go ahead.

"Booker, I'm afraid the colored man has lost the best man they ever had," Dad said. "It's gonna hurt whites, too, the loss of Dr. King. Booker, if you wish to go to church, I understand. If you wish to knock off with your crew, I'll cover at the office."

Booker declined the offer. "Thank you for that, but we'll work," he said. "We'll pick."

Dad said he could feel the eyes of the men following him

as he walked back to his car. That was it. Martin Luther King Jr. was dead, and there were seven more hours of picking that day.

"If I had gotten out there like an old blowhard, I would have ruined my relationship with Booker," Dad said to Mom. But if his boss found out that he'd offered to let Booker's crew knock off early, there'd be hell to pay. Dad did not have the authority to make such an offer.

He stayed out on the porch by himself a long time that night, coming in every now and then to refill his glass.

After Dr. King was assassinated, the newspaper put the story at the bottom of the front page. The main headline was: WE HAVE A NEW MISS SEBRING.

CHAPTER 9

The night before Easter Sunday, we had to go to bed early and stay there. Late at night I thought I heard my parents in the kitchen. It was April and all the windows were open. I heard a metal ice tray crack against the edge of the kitchen counter. My father was reading instructions out loud to my mother, something about how to give an egg a bath.

The next morning, the house was silent. The door to my bedroom was closed. When I swung out of my bed, my feet knocked something over. A purple Easter basket, filled with plastic grass and jelly beans and malted milk eggs. I was appraising the goods that had spilled on the rug when I noticed an amazing thing. Someone had arranged a diorama of figures on the floor. A brigade of chocolate rabbits standing in a circle and in the middle was a family of Peeps. The yellow spongy chicks with dot eyes were looking up at milk chocolate rabbits. If ever there were a time to believe in fairies and Easter bunnies, it would have been then. The elaborate Easter scene had been built with care and precision. My father must have done this. Remembering the noise from last night, I went to the kitchen.

An empty bottle of Imperial whiskey was on the counter next to the sink. Broken eggshells in different colors were on the counter. No one was in the living room, but an album cover was on the couch, one I had never seen. Herb Alpert and the Tijuana Brass. *Whipped Cream & Other Delights*. I picked it up. There was a voluptuous brunette, naked, dressed only in whipped cream, and she was licking some of the cream off.

I don't know how long I had been staring at the album cover when I heard my father in the kitchen making coffee. The sun outside was already burning through the living room window. It was a hot morning for a neighborhood egg hunt.

All the kids had to stay inside their houses while the fathers hid the eggs. They ordered us to stay away from the window, but I pulled back the curtain. Dad was dragging. He was doing what he was supposed to do, placing a colored egg here or there in the grass, but without much imagination. He left two eggs by the swing set pole and they weren't even hidden very well.

Our neighbor Mr. Navarro had a new Polaroid Swinger and wanted a group photo outside. The boys used the time to scan for Easter eggs, their eyes darting around as they mapped their attack. The girls looked at Mr. Navarro's camera and smiled when he said smile. If an egg hunt with prizes didn't interest them, what ever would? Clutching my Easter egg basket, I bolted across the yard like a crazed prospector. The first stop was the swing set for an easy two. I made a frenzied run along the fence lines, shrub to shrub, sweat trickling, all elbows, collecting egg after egg. The other kids lacked precision—they had not cheated by looking out the window.

My only real competition was a boy who was a year older.

At the exact same moment, we both saw the pink egg balanced on a tree stump. We charged, neck and neck all the way until suddenly he went down, a terrible crash. I heard my father shout my name, the same way he shouted our dog Helene's name after she snatched the Salisbury steak off my brother's TV dinner tray. ANNE!

The rest of the egg hunt was spent sitting on top of twenty-pound bags of Purina dog chow in the carport as punishment for knocking the kid down. When all the eggs were gone, my father came over and described the virtues of sharing. He said next year he hoped for better. He said I had to set a good example for my brother. I saw Dwight sitting in the yard by himself eating the egg he had found. You didn't have to teach him; he was born nice. My father said go in and get ready, we're going up to see Big Nanny.

BIG NANNY was the matriarch, my father's grandmother and Gigi's mother-in-law. She was so high up the Hull totem pole she didn't live in Hopewell anymore. She and her husband, Papa, had lived in the big house for decades but recently moved into Plant City proper, shaving six miles off the trip to their doctors. It was a ranch house in a neighborhood of ranch houses, as sterile and sun-beaten as Hopewell was lush and ancient. But it had central air-conditioning that was good for Papa's breathing.

Even before we loaded into the car, my father was chain-smoking. He tried to time our departure so that we'd be pulling into Big Nanny's driveway as everyone arrived there from church. He thought if we dressed up we would blend in with the crowd. We were on a mission—we weren't going for the ham and sweet potatoes.

My father pulled at his necktie the whole way. The wind whipped through the open windows like oven heat. The road from Sebring to Big Nanny's was empty, and by then I knew the way. "That's Bartow," I said to Dwight, when we came through the white phosphate pits. He looked out the window. The wind fluttered back his blond hair. We drove on. The backs of my bare legs stuck to the gritty car seat as if glued down. Big Nanny liked to see young ladies in dresses.

We got there windblown and covered in a sheen. Big Nanny was waiting at the door. "Well, bless your heart, come on in," she said, turning on her aluminum walker.

The kitchen was small with two feet of countertop. Big Nanny gave up real cooking when she and Papa moved into town. It was an old person's kitchen, but on Sunday when the relatives made their pilgrimage, it turned into a buffet of warm casserole dishes. The younger women angled for space as they pulled off the tinfoil.

The one thing Big Nanny still made was her famous fudge. She needed a magnifying glass to find the wooden spoon on the counter. The magnifying glass would fog with the detritus of human breath and spittle, but a few hours later, a perfect pan of fudge was cooling on a rack. Big Nanny had her girl cut the fudge in little squares and store it in a kitchen drawer lined with wax paper. Kids weren't allowed to open the fudge drawer. It opened and closed on metal rollers, making for a very distinctive sound. I was fixated on getting inside that drawer.

When Big Nanny was in the other room and I was by myself in the kitchen, I'd get it open two or three inches and Big Nanny would call from the other room, "Is that you in the kitchen?"

You had to be alert for any opportunity that arose.

Another time we visited Big Nanny, she asked if I would like for her to read the Bible to me.

"Yes, ma'am, from Papa's special Bible?" I knew Papa's Bible was in her bedroom on her lacquered white night table. This delighted Big Nanny to no end. As she shuffled off to her bedroom, I hurried to the fudge drawer.

On Easter, the house was too full of people for any such scheme. Eating lunch took a half hour; the sitting around part lasted for hours. Conversation—about oranges, Sunday school, the sale price on fryers, University of Alabama football—floated on an endless metronomic cloud of time. There were periods of silence, where everyone seemed to be chewing over what the last person said, until the next one said, "I reckon so."

Big Nanny adored my father. You could see it in how she looked at him with her watery blue squid eyes. She patted his arm differently than the others. Maybe she felt bad about the way her son, my father's father, left his family early when he drank himself to death. At some point that afternoon, she made a big show of going to her rolltop desk, where she kept her checkbook.

"John, honey, you want to come with me?" she said as she made the long journey to the desk fifteen feet away, leaning on her walker. After great effort to get there, she sat down in her chair with a heavy sigh and opened the big leather-bound ledger, really taking her time. "Now, let me see," she said, pulling a drawer open. She fuddled around for an ink pen. My father had to just stand there while Big Nanny held the magnifying glass over the check so she could see. At last, there was the sound of perforated paper being torn from its moorings.

Papa rested after dinner. I liked studying him while he rested, so I went over to the vibrating reclining chair. He looked like a baby ghost, translucent and white, with a few angel wisps of hair on his head. Big Nanny dressed him in ironed khakis and leather shoes that laced up like he was going somewhere, but he just stayed levitating like a vibrating plank in his recliner. His recliner was a first-generation vibrating model with the turbo of a Boeing 747. The control panel was on the armrest. The TV tray beside him was stacked with Florida Citrus Mutual newsletters and appeals from Baptist missionaries. It was all for show; Papa couldn't read anymore.

"Read for Papa," the relatives told me. I picked up one of the missionary letters and read to Papa about how the African children were giving up witchcraft for Scripture.

I leaned in close to his ear. "Papa, can I switch you on high?" I asked. He responded with a faint smile. Within seconds we had liftoff. Papa's eyes jiggled in their watery sockets and coins shook loose from his pockets, falling onto the terrazzo floor. My father came over and switched him to low. He said tell everyone bye, we were leaving. Big Nanny stood at the garage door on her walker and waved. She wasn't fat except for her arms and they were all extra meat. "Come back, hear?" she called out, waving. The folded check was in my father's shirt pocket.

Big Nanny was probably a nice lady, but I couldn't really say. Adults flicker around us, coming in and out of our awakening consciousness. Big Nanny was the person we went to see for money. We'd be going back more and more.

CHAPTER 10

We left Sebring after first grade and moved twice in two years, each move bringing us closer to Big Nanny.

By the time we moved to Plant City just before my third-grade year, my father was sinking fast.

My mother did not teach that year. She traded in her career for Sunday afternoon processionals to Big Nanny's and the intricate coordination over which wife would bring what covered dish. "Is it all right with everybody if I sprinkle the Durkee's crispy onions on top of the green bean casserole, or do y'all prefer it without?" These were the burning questions of the day.

When our tires ga-thumped over glazed brick streets from the horse and buggy days, I knew we were in Plant City. Our new home was on Reynolds Street. After more ga-thumping, we came to a big grassy lot on the corner, and Dad turned in.

"This ain't ours," I said, looking at the humongous house.

"Isn't ours," my mother said, reaching for the door handle.

The elegant wood frame house was two stories high with

stone steps out front. Inside, the ceilings reached celestial heights. The doorknobs were made of glass. There were two fireplaces, one downstairs and one up, but what took the cake was the chandelier in the foyer. It was a twinkling crystal bomb, the sun and the moon combined, with beads and ornate drippings. Suddenly we had a chandelier. The house had to be my father's idea. "Arrive in a good car and good suit and doors will open," he liked to say. He must have needed a few doors to open.

THE HEAT that first day was wicked. Every time my mother opened one of the big heavy windows with the sash-type rope pulleys, they made a ferocious noise like a castle drawbridge being raised. She hoisted one after another. My father was irritable and guzzling coffee from his work thermos as he left out the back door. Boxes and newspapers were everywhere. I saw my mother wade into a pile in the living room. She dragged her walnut-grain Magnavox stereo console across the oak floor. She was going to play her music. Here she was unpacking yet another house. She tied a scarf in her hair and set the needle down on *Fiddler on the Roof*.

She started in the kitchen. On her hands and knees, wiping out cabinets, lining shelves with contact paper. With Comet in one hand and a scrub brush in the other, she went after the rust marks in the old farm sink and a red countertop where fifty years of biscuits were probably rolled out by the loving hands of a wife humming "How Great Thou Art."

"If I Were a Rich Man" pretty much vanquished that history. Suddenly it was a Russian shtetl, the madness of clarinets and violins at gale force. With her rag and her scarf, my mother looked the part. She sang along with the score. "Hodel, oh Hodel, have I made a match for you!" Periodically she would wander out to the living room, and each time the volume got a little louder.

Midmorning, when my father reappeared, she turned up the burner underneath a pot of coffee on the stove. He must have come up the back steps. Sweat prickled his forehead and a silver tire gauge was in his hand, the kind gas station men kept in their shirt pocket. He pointed toward the stereo. "You might like to turn that down before the neighbors call the law," he said.

"Coffee?" she asked.

The tire gauge went skittering across the counter. "What I would like is a modicum of sensitivity to the situation," he replied. Once, he found ethnic music exotic. Now, a band of hollering Russian peasants at eleven o'clock in the morning was not putting the best foot forward with the new neighbors. He asked my mother if she was trying to make a statement, but he didn't wait for the answer. He grabbed his tire gauge and strode into the living room. He slammed the window so hard the dishes in the cabinet rattled.

In a flash my mother was at the Magnavox lifting up the needle. Every note of sound was sucked from the air. "John," she said, turning back to face my father, "it's from *Broadway*."

My father rubbed his eyes. The house stayed silent for a while. Later they reconnoitered on the back porch, as if they communicated via some wordless bandwidth. My father was sitting on top of the washing machine. My mother leaned against the screen door, the lush green of the yard behind her, her scarf now in her hand as she folded it into tighter and tighter triangles. Soon the music came back on.

Paper plates wobbled on our knees as we ate our lunch. The afternoon sun blasted through the curtainless windows. *Man of La Mancha* was winding down with Don Quixote wailing on about the impossible dream, and my father chewed peaceably. He said my bologna sandwiches were the best he ever had, and if he could eat this good every day, he would sure as hell brown-bag it. My mother had cleared junk off the couch so she had a place to sit, and she ate as she looked through a J.C. Penney catalog with women in gaucho pants and desert blouses, their hair blowing free in the wind.

I felt alone with my observations. I walked around the new house that first day, discovering a windowsill full of bug skeletons and carrying a special clipboard with a golf pencil attached to keep track of all the things I wanted—a Girl Scout rain poncho, a diary with a lock, and a shortwave radio.

DWIGHT AND I were as different as two children from the same parents could be, but my father had done a clever thing. By calling me "Sister" and Dwight "Brother," he tied us together, one connection to be cashed in when the time was right.

After lunch, he asked us to come outside to the front yard. He said he wanted us to learn our new address. His idea was to have us stand in the broiling sun and stare at the house numbers. Say it, children: 508 East Reynolds Street. This old house had a history. He said it had been on this corner for as long as he could remember, even before when he was a little boy. It was known as the old Austin house, after the doctor who lived there for decades, but really it went back to 1919 to a Mrs. Evelyn Crum and her prosperous businessman husband, who decided to copy a Cape Cod–style house they had seen up north.

An unusual brightness came into Dwight's eyes. "We live in the old Crum house," he said. The thrill of his pun drove him to the ground in laughter. He stayed on his back like a bug. My father regarded him with bemusement.

I studied the white house, such a grand old dowager, its shadow looming, swallowing us whole. Downtown was apparently a few blocks west on Reynolds Street, but I saw no sign of the lively Plant City my father had talked up. Behind us on the corner was a mechanic's garage with cars up on blocks.

Dwight and I sat down on the steps, a half-moon of chiseled stone, while my father remained standing. He told us how much we would enjoy our new town. He said the start of the new school year would bring opportunities to meet new friends. I asked if the Strawberry Festival was ever moved up earlier in the year. He said no, the tradition was February and that's how it had been since 1930. He took all our questions, in no rush to go back inside. He tore into the foil on his new pack of Dentyne and offered us both a stick.

As the cinnamon fire burned in our mouths, he squatted down on the walkway to get level with us. His voice was calm as he put his eyes on me. "Sister, I want you to look after Brother," he said.

It was a burden I did not want. Worse, it sounded like an advance storm warning, something was out there and it was coming for us. Dwight had stood up to bat grasshoppers off a shrub.

"You mean right now?" I asked my father.

"Always," my father said, smiling.

"What about my lemonade business?"

"I'm not talking about babysitting Brother," he said, in a non-condescending voice, which I appreciated. "Your mama and I depend on you to be a strong girl."

That night Dwight and I went to look at the fireplace in our parents' bedroom. Neither of us had ever seen a fireplace inside a house. This one had green ceramic tiles. What caught my eye was the emptiness of the room, the bare mattress, and the unpacked boxes. Maybe they were saving their room for last. Dwight and I sat down in front of the fireplace. Cool air pushed out from the darkness. "Are those from Mrs. Crum?" Dwight asked.

"What?" I said.

"The ashes."

I told him I didn't think ashes survived that long and they were probably from other people. He jumped up and said he'd be right back. Five minutes later he charged up the stairs with two sticks and marshmallows on the end. "Don't trip and stab yourself," I said, taking mine at the top of the stairs.

"How can I, with a marshmallow on the end?" he asked with obvious pride and a smug, lopsided smile.

Cross-legged, our knees touching, we held our sticks over an imaginary campfire. "It's getting hot," Dwight said. "Is yours done?"

"Mine needs another second," I said, rotating my stick.

There could be only one explanation for a house with two fireplaces. Big Nanny must have kicked in on the down payment to buy it. All the inexplicable phenomena in our lives could be traced back to Big Nanny. She was the shadow hand behind the curtain. She had that old Hopewell pioneer stock in her, and even though she pushed Ephesians 2:8 on me and was not exactly forthcoming with her fudge, she was solid. I was glad for the backup.

Years later, I went looking for information about that time in our lives. I learned that Big Nanny had not bought the Reynolds Street house for us. By then, the "principals" were all gone. That's the term the clerk at the county property office used for the deceased—my parents—whose names should have surfaced on a bill of sale or a deed transfer. Not a single file came up, not a sliver of microfilm.

I did get the name of a man who once owned the house. When I called him at home, he answered the way people do in Plant City, with an elongated "hello," an upswing on the second syllable, like a musical question mark. The man was very old. He was also very sharp. He ticked off buyers and sellers going back four decades. How dumb could I have been. We never owned the house. By the time we got to Plant City, our footprint had lightened considerably. We were renters.

The day we moved into the house, I knew we didn't belong there. It was that damn chandelier. I refused to walk under it. It's just a light, my father said; it won't hurt you.

The first night was worse than the first day. Sleeping in a house made of old wood was spooky. My bedroom was upstairs on the corner, hanging off the ledge of darkness, creaking and groaning all night long. We were a boat lost at sea, tilting and keeling in the dark, and water was seeping through the slats. In the morning my bed was wet.

Everyone said it was an aberration but that turned out not to be the case. On the second night, the house heaved and groaned and the sea came into my bed again. This went on for nearly a week. My mother scrubbed my mattress with bleach and propped it against the window to air. Seeing the faint yellow amoeba shapes in daylight, I pretended they were someone else's malfunctions. When my mother came home from the store with plastic bedding, it was clear we were crossing into more permanent territory. A latex sheet was hard to deny. I was eight years old and peeing the bed.

My father kept a Florida Spray Man's calendar next to the phone so he could jot down his business thoughts. The thing was awash in numbers and tonnage rates and stick figures hanging by a noose, but I could see that it was August. Soon I'd be starting third grade at my new school. I was terrified I would reek of urine. At night in bed I'd try to hypnotize myself into staying awake, focusing on an object the way Illya Kuryakin did on *The Man from U.N.C.L.E.* My eyes burned, and then they closed.

Every last trick was exhausted. No liquids after dinner. My father explained the properties of wood boards, the expansion and contraction that naturally occur with temperature change. Wood is a living thing, he said. That only made things worse. I started seeing faces on my bedroom wall. He tried to be solicitous the morning after a deluge, though he was squeamish on matters of female biology. Was the extra nightlight helping any? Should I swap bedrooms with Brother? What we're dealing with here, he said, is a simple case of relocation jitters. He also said something about every pony needing to get used to its pasture.

He doled out the adages while I sat on the edge of the bathtub in the morning watching him spit Listerine or knock his razor against the sink. We'd go downstairs for breakfast, where damp sheets partitioned off the kitchen. I had convinced my mother to hang the sheets inside the laundry room and kitchen instead of broadcasting my troubles on the clothesline. It was a scene from *The Grapes of Wrath* when the Joads were in the Okie camp, with Dwight and me spooning our grub on one side of a sheet while smoke from my father's cigarette rose up on the other side.

The crisis did wonders for my parents. My mother stopped checking her gold Timex watch as she got dinner ready and my father glided home from work just as the meatloaf was coming out of the oven. They were like two Olympic skaters reunited, synched up and hitting their marks like the old days. All it took was my plastic sheets.

Then came the inevitable morning when I woke up in a dry bed. I should have been happy that I wouldn't be starting third grade at my new school smelling like a cat box. Instead I was already nostalgic for the plastic sheets and their miraculous powers over my father's sobriety. What would happen now that the crisis might be passing? There was only one thing to do, but before I did it, I savored the joy of that dry bed, the sheets so light and airy and unstuck together by the dungeon dampness, the scent of spring and lambs and clover and bleach. Then I opened the floodgates, and thanked God for plastic sheets.

* * *

ONE EVENING my father said that Gigi was coming over to babysit. She lived by herself in a cement block house a few blocks away with her dog Topper and a white piano. It was showcased in her front room like a pearl-handled gun, a far cry from the black uprights the Hopewell relatives used for hymns. Gigi didn't mix a lot with the Hopewell crowd anymore.

We needed a babysitter because my parents were going to dinner at the Red Barn. It was on a beat-up road going to Lakeland but inside was velvet-type wallpaper and good steaks. That meant the possibility of leftover steak in the fridge in the morning. A lot could be gleaned from how much was left over. A few scraps that needed to be coated in butter—they had a nice time. An entire steak untouched and wrapped in foil meant their nice time got ruined somehow.

My father put on a tie in front of the mirror. "Be good for Mama," he said as he made a knot.

"Ain't she going with you," I said, trying to have fun with him.

"You know what I mean," he said, sweeping the change off the top of his dresser into his hand. "Be sweet with her. She's not used to children."

That got my attention, a possible irregularity that maybe just slipped out. As I understood it, Gigi had two children and one of them was standing in front of me. "You and Aunt Anne, weren't y'all her kids?" I said.

He paused in thought. "That was a long time ago," he said. He picked through his coins and gave me a quarter. Then he went looking for Dwight.

"Are you giving him a quarter too?" I yelled. I would never get ahead in this house.

Gigi arrived on time with a book and a carton of Tarey-
tons.

She parked in back and came in through the kitchen. She
was stealthy, soft around the middle with short legs, but
she seemed to move on air. After my parents left, she went to
the fridge and poured herself a glass of tea. My mother had
left a note on the counter with emergency phone numbers for
the pediatrician, but Gigi set her sweating glass of iced tea
right down on it while she looked for the sugar bowl. I watched
her heap five or six tablespoons of sugar into the glass. She
was fascinating. She would cut her eyes at me sideways and
smile, a Southern coquette who was more of a little girl than
me, and I was an actual little girl. She exuded passivity and
deference, and yet there I was trotting behind her as she pad-
ded out to the living room. "Honey, do you want to watch
a show with me?" she asked, but she was only trying to be
polite. She opened her book.

I sat on the stairs. Through the spindles in the banister, I
could see her. Whenever she went to the kitchen to refill her
tea, she came back with the white crystal tornado of sugar
swirling in the glass. She smoked like a fiend and read with
intensity. She would root around in her pocketbook for a
piece of hard candy now and then but was semi-oblivious
to the two grandchildren in her care. Not even the incessant
buzzing from Dwight's room could pique her interest. He was
playing Operation and losing badly. "Don't let your tweezers
touch," I called up. "You're gonna wear out the battery."

I must have dozed off on the stairs. Groggily, I looked
down at my case study. She was still in the chair reading, the
lamp pointed on her book like an interrogation light. She

totally blanked on our bedtime. I went upstairs to Dwight's room. He was asleep on the floor with the lights blazing and little pieces of Operation anatomy scattered everywhere.

To combat the August heat, I'd developed a system to ease my thirst. It involved soaking the sleeves and collar of my pajamas with water. That way when I got thirsty, I could just suck on my pajamas. I was standing at the sink, doing my soaking routine, when Gigi appeared in the doorway. She had come up the stairs on her silent cat feet.

"Well, what on earth?" she asked, suddenly a babysitter.

I found out that she reported me to the higher-ups, though not for the obvious crime. It was her opinion that a young lady of eight was too old for pajamas. "It's getting to be that time for a nightgown," she told my father the following day. This was how his people talked when they were trying to pry you loose from your happy ways and nudge you toward things like dance lessons. You couldn't just grow up. You had to make a series of time-appropriate concessions. Everything was a rite of passage. They showered you with soft white leather Bibles and antique dolls and bookends shaped like praying hands.

All I wanted was an air gun.

TWO DAYS later I was sitting in Gigi's bedroom in the middle of the afternoon. She had invited me over for a surprise. She led me down her dimly lit hallway into her bedroom. The blinds were three-quarters closed, almost blocking out all sunlight. What light came through illuminated the trillion motes of dust that hung in the air. Tortoise hair combs, brooches, and pearl cameos were arranged on the white lace that covered the top of her dresser. As I opened one of the cameos, Gigi came out of the bathroom wearing a negligee.

Burned into my memory for eternity was that vision. The nightgown was long and satiny and emerald colored. The slippers were the same color with two-inch heels. Gigi looked like she was going to a prom in bed. She modeled the gown with catlike grace, a real floor show, turning this way and that, placing a hand on her hip. I sat frozen on the edge of her hard bed. The emerald nightie was just the beginning. Gigi modeled nightgowns and peignoir sets, a whole slew of bantamweight frocks with satin piping and ribbon trim.

"Now," she said, when it was all over and the gowns were on her bed. "Aren't these marvelous?"

"Yes, ma'am," I said, steeling myself for what was to come.

Yet she made no effort to lobby the merits of the nightgown. She was in her own world, content, drifting. I watched her fold the last of her nightgowns in tissue and close the drawer. She went to the kitchen for her iced tea and a bag of Pecan Sandies, brought everything back to her bedroom, and switched on the TV. With the blinds closed, the TV glowed like a movie screen. She extended the delicate saucer with the fleur-de-lis pattern in my direction. "Sandie?" she asked. For the next half hour, we watched *Dark Shadows* without speaking. I never heard another word about a nightgown.

CHAPTER 11

It was 1969 in Plant City, but it felt like 1949. The drug-store downtown still served three-course lunches and you ate your roast turkey and giblets next to a spinner rack of ladies' hosiery. Plant City wasn't old-fashioned; it was against the future. A bank in town had recently unveiled a new sign that used digital numbers to show the time and temperature. It was seen as a stunt and largely ignored by a town that pre-ferred the big fat hands of time, "like Hillsboro State Bank does it."

Every Tuesday night at 7:25, I went around the house tell-ing everyone to keep it quiet and don't disturb me, *The Mod Squad* was about to come on. I was fully invested in the lives of the three hippie detectives—"One Black, One White, One Blonde"—who drove around in the front seat together with their legs touching.

The next morning, I was back in Plant City, where the local chapter of the United Daughters of the Confederacy released their new cookbook.

It was a love of history and heritage, everyone said, but when I was born at the town hospital eight years earlier, the maternity ward was white only, and Black women were sent to a separate area called the Carver wing. The year before, when Hurricane Donna knocked out the power, the white side had generators and the Carver wing did not. The hospital wouldn't budge, no Blacks in the maternity ward, so a white obstetrician named Hal Brewer rigged up enough light to see what he was doing and delivered a Black baby in the smothering heat of the Carver wing.

Maybe the focus on heritage was compensation for Plant City's humble origins, described in one history book as "350 people, wandering hogs and no money." The place was surrounded by strawberry fields and orange groves, but inside some of the bigger houses were pewter ambrosia cups and ball gowns dying for any occasion to be brought out. You could feel the longing for a social register. On Reynolds Street, our house was across from where a man named Jim Walter had grown up. Jim Walter became a millionaire home builder. The house was a decrepit eyesore with a bunch of shovels and hoes on the porch, but anytime someone learned where I lived, they'd clasp their hands and say, "Oh, you must be near the Walter home."

"Yes, ma'am, we're right near there," I said, playing along, because that's what everyone did here.

I was zoned for Stonewall Jackson Elementary, and when my mother went to school to register me, she saw the portrait of the bearded Confederate general in the hallway. She questioned my father about the Confederate love stuff. He said it was probably hard for a Northerner to understand. He was right about that part. Around the time I started fourth grade at Stonewall Jackson, a local Black man sat at a lunch counter downtown and tried ordering a hamburger. He was brought a plate of raw meat.

STONEWALL JACKSON Elementary was brand-new, with state-of-the art windows along the tops of the classroom walls to maximize air flow. For the first time, Jackson was forced to share some of its good sweet air with a Black student. The county school board had spent the last eight years fighting court-ordered integration and finally had exhausted all legal avenues. The new student, a second grader named Pauline, was in my friend Dixie's class.

"She's the sweetest girl," Dixie reported. "Real quiet, real nice."

Dixie was a girl who enjoyed her pork chops, and I was a girl who liked to wear pants, two factors which set us off to the side from the ideal. We sat together at lunch every day. We both found the food to be superb. Mrs. Cotton, the cafeteria manager, ran her kitchen like a culinary institute. She must have had the ladies frying drumsticks by hand. All morning the smell of biscuits wafted into the classroom. Just the smell made me touch the thirty-five cents in my pocket for a lunch ticket.

The roar of the lunchroom could get pretty loud. If the volume reached a certain level, the principal or her assistant rang a small handbell as a warning. Scofflaws were sent to the office where a paddle hung on a hook. I never took the wood, but it was only luck. At lunch, Dixie and I packed our straws with beets or carrots or whatever mushy vegetable was left on our tray and blew beet darts at the wall pygmy-style.

On hot days, after those heavy lunches, kids started dropping around one o'clock. You'd hear the sound of the janitors' keys swinging from their belts as they rushed to the latest casualty, wielding mops and buckets of pine-scented sawdust that wicked away the hot stench of vomit. That's what afternoons at Stonewall Jackson Elementary smelled like: biscuits and vomit sprinkle. Dixie and I never barfed, though we should have.

CEOLA'S NAME, her real name, was written on a notepad on the kitchen counter in my father's blocky handwriting: THEORA JONES. The name seemed out of place in Plant City. Ceola and Clarence didn't have a phone while we were in Sebring. They must have put one in.

I tried her a number of times, but no one answered. One day, I called later than usual and she picked up.

"Ceola, it's me," I said.

"Who is this?" she said.

"It's Anne, the girl you used to stay with!"

"Wait, now," she said. "You say who now?" Some irritation crept into her voice.

I didn't know how to remind her who I was. If she had forgotten me, why did I remember her? The silence got louder, like a sinkhole spreading wider, and I hung up quick before it took me down.

ONE SATURDAY out of the blue my father announced that it was time for me to ride my bike downtown on my own. My mother was against it. My father spoke on behalf of children worldwide when he said, "Vicki, this is how they learn."

He was in the front yard wearing tan pants, so he must have been on his way to work. I had my bike on the grass.

"This sidewalk will take you downtown," he said, pointing at the thin strip of concrete in the grass.

It was a revelation of major import. I'd been downtown once, by car, with my mother to buy light bulbs at McCrory's. I had never seen such a place. A lady in uniform was tending a popcorn machine. There were two aisles of toys, heavy on the pistols and light on the dolls. Balloons were strung over the lunch counter. I had heard at school that inside each balloon was a folded-up piece of paper scrawled with a number.

Places that good took a car ride to get to. I looked down at the crumble of concrete. "This sidewalk?" I asked.

"Stand here," my father said.

I looked down the street as far as I could. The view revealed nothing. Ordinary houses lined the street. Oak trees dripped their mossy beards. A warm weight settled on my shoulder. My father's hand. It stayed there as we both looked in the direction of downtown.

Dad told me a story. When he was my age, he had a lawn-mowing business. One day he got an idea. He was dirty from cutting grass and wanted a steak. He showered, put on his church suit, and called the only cab in Plant City. He told the driver to take him to Combs' café downtown.

"I had a steak, the whole works," he said, grinning proudly. "Well, I came up short when the check arrived, and there was cussing and hollering."

Standing next to me on the sidewalk, he laughed, jingling the coins in his pocket.

The hook was in. I had to go downtown.

"You know to look both ways before you cross," he said, holding on to my bike handle. "And when you see people, speak to them. This is your town."

I was eager to get going, and then my mother came out on the front steps, probably trying to squash the trip.

"Can you pick up a stick of butter?" she called out.

"Ha ha," I said. When I glanced back, she was in the doorway, watching me.

"Wait," my father said. One arm disappeared behind him, reaching for his wallet. He pulled out a five-dollar bill, which I quickly snatched. He started saying something else, some final word of wisdom, but I was already pedaling.

NO SOONER had I become an independent voyager able to travel great distances on my own than the conventions of girlhood finally caught up to me.

The Girl Scouts met at the Brownie Hut in Plant City. I wanted a house like the Brownie Hut. It was made of logs and it had a fireplace and smelled of woodsmoke. The refrigerator was stocked with jugs of fruit punch and Girl Scout cookies, and inside the door was a bottle of Mylanta in case anyone got a sour stomach. What else did you need?

We weren't allowed to go to the pond outside the Brownie Hut because of water moccasins. It added to our sense of adventure, knowing that a tangle of serpents was on the other side of the door as we stood to give the Pledge of Allegiance. My friend Dixie and I planned out which badges we wanted to earn for our sashes. We all brought in recipes from home and we mimeographed them and stapled them together. One girl brought a recipe for Dr Pepper cake, another brought "grandma's peach pie," and my contribution was a recipe for sukiyaki.

Dixie possessed a wide array of Brownie gear and accouterments. She came to meetings with an olive-green mess kit with a cup, plate, and spoon inside. Her pretend world had a wider range than mine. She raided her older sister's closet for go-go boots and sequin tops to dress up as one of Dean Martin's Golddigger dancers. Her sister went on to become the Plant City Strawberry Queen, high royalty in town. Her sister shared stories of getting her hair done at the Wig Box, where the curling irons plugged into the ceiling. Dixie didn't consider herself Strawberry Queen material. Pork chops and caramel cake were too dear to her, but she basked in the glory of being kin to royalty.

PLANT CITY had been struck by the tap-dancing craze. The hub of tap lessons was Jackie's School of Dance. On the days I wasn't at Gigi's after school or at the Brownie Hut with Dixie, I was at Jackie's. The studio was on the second floor of an old building on Reynolds Street downtown. The owner, Miss Jackie, had studied with a ballet company up north, and this created a waiting list with local mothers wanting their girls to "study" under Miss Jackie.

Every Tuesday afternoon, I trudged up the stairs carrying my tap shoes. Inside, a dozen eight-year-olds wearing rouge were already clicking around on the polished floor. I hated the sound; it made me anxious and rushed as I put on my shoes. My hair wasn't long enough to put in a bun. For the next thirty minutes, I tried not to slip. I kept trying to make it to the strip of carpet that led to the bathroom. Nervous sweat burned through my leotard, making wet circles under my arms.

After my successful bike trip downtown, I wanted to ride my bike to Gladys Jeffcoat's photography studio instead. Gladys specialized in family portraits, but her passion was photographing car wrecks. She had a police scanner and she often beat the *Tampa Tribune* or the *Lakeland Ledger* photographer to the scene. Clicking around on the floor seemed like a huge waste of time, and I was terrible at it. Then my father told me something important about Jackie's School of Dance. He said Jackie's School of Dance had a float in the grand parade during the Plant City Strawberry Festival and her girls rode on it. That was incentive enough to stay with tap. The parade was always on the first Monday in March. For two months we rehearsed in our clicking shoes and crafted wands out of Reynolds aluminum wrap and special-ordered leotards. In the event of a cold snap, we were to wear white or cream sweaters only.

Miss Jackie had instructed us to meet her at the JSOD float near Kilgore Seed and to arrive ready—hair, face, tights, the works. At home I'd stood in the bathroom stiff as a board while my mother dug around in her makeup drawers for lipstick and blush. She sat on the edge of the white claw-foot tub. Think of it as Halloween, she said, without the Pink Panther costume. She tried to keep a straight face as she applied my lipstick. I drew the line at eye shadow.

Miss Jackie assured us there would be room for our whole class on the float. That's how good-hearted she was. She also knew the Darwinian frenzy that occurred when three dozen females in rouge stepped on a parade float. Nature would sort itself out.

School was canceled the day of the parade. Businesses were closed. My father had left the house early to attend the prayer breakfast for town leaders at First Baptist Church. Over eggs, bacon, biscuits, and watery coffee, the state agriculture commissioner promised a banner year for Florida citrus. The floats began streaming into town from the barns and pastures where they'd been decorated in secret. Seeing them for the first time was exciting. The churches roped pianos and organs on top of their floats; everyone else used canned music over tinny bullhorns. One of the car dealerships was already playing "A Boy Named Sue."

Our float was midway back in the parade lineup. Miss Jackie always went all out. A crepe paper fringe swept the bottom of the float, like a hula skirt, and on top, big letters spelled out JSOD. About thirty of us climbed aboard and spread out. The prettiest girls jostled to get out front as the public face. I made a beeline for the anonymous middle. I didn't want unknown masses in lawn chairs scrutinizing every inch of me. My preference was not to be seen at all. The prestige of riding on the float was good enough. I already had a small hole in my white tights from scrambling on board.

Our mandate was to tap-dance the entire one-mile parade route. Between the lipstick and the hair, we looked like pageant contestants eager for the runway. The exhaust from the idling engines made us glossy. Finally, it was time, and the floats began to roll.

Our first girl tapped off the edge of the float after a few blocks. We kept rolling until someone yelled at the driver and the float jerked to a halt. Miss Jackie came running over. The girl was fine. They brushed her off, redid her bun, and we got back into the flow.

We moved beneath archways of Spanish moss. People lined the streets. They tilted their faces up in benevolent appreciation. The Baptists sat together on one side of the street and the Methodists sat together on the other. They gave their full attention to each float. The stars of the parade were the Strawberry Queen and her court, five young women who were the most beautiful daughters of the town scions. The queen wore a three-pound silver crown. Men took off their hats and women beamed, imagining themselves on the float.

Cynicism had no place in their hearts. Unwrapping the wax paper from the sandwiches they brought from home, they did it without looking so they wouldn't miss a second of the parade that only happened once a year, and though they had never missed a single one, this was the best one yet. The floats moved slowly. There was no hurry. Go on and make it last forever.

CHAPTER 12

The magnitude of the groves always took outsiders by surprise. Especially in March and April, when the orange blossoms turned the Ridge into an open-air perfume counter. But to drive nine hundred miles in a salt-caked vehicle just to see an orange?

They clogged the highways getting down to us. There was something about picking their own orange that they liked, and they liked taking pictures of themselves doing it. Women in skimpy shorts on ladders arched their backs.

If they happened to take State Road 60, they were headed straight for the groves at Hopewell. A few miles out they'd start to see my great aunt Dot's signs hammered into the trees and propped in the grass.

HULL GROVES/FLORIDA'S SWEETEST NAVELS,
500 YARDS AHEAD!!!!
FRESH-SQUEEZED, YOU WON'T BE SORRY!!!!
START BRAKING NOW!!!!

Aunt Dot did her own advertising for the Hull Groves family fruit stand at the edge of our groves. She used five-by-five-foot sheets of plywood and painted urgent messages on them in tent revival boldface. She said good visibility and a little bragging helped lure in motorists. The common strategy of roadside advertising was to pummel the wayfarers through hypnotic repetition. Not Aunt Dot's—Dot's signs were unique outcries of passion. Even from a car going sixty-five miles per hour, each sign was a fresh jolt to the senses.

The apocalyptic signage put a certain mental picture in the minds of the travelers. They expected to see a fruit stand in a ring of fire. Instead they came to a wood plank box in a small clearing. Never had there been a more somber admonishment than the Hull Groves fruit stand. Not a single gold hinge glinted from its timber face. The roof was a sheet of aluminum and the floors were dirt. It looked like Abe Lincoln might be sleeping inside. Our fruit stand was a rebuke to modernity and the Yankees who had expected something more. When they pulled onto the grass out front, they sat in their cars and stared.

Dot had black eyes and had grown up going to primitive Baptist camp meetings in the woods. When she married Uncle Roy, my father's uncle, she went to his indoor church, twice on Sunday and once on Wednesday night. Even so, she wore lipstick, a shade she called Drug Store Red. The fruit stand awakened a deep zest in her—for the hustle, for the money, for the chance to hear the different ways people talked. Maybe it was the closeness of the highway or the ring of the cash register, but around Dot, you felt the thrill of the game.

"Aunt Dot, some are here!" I called out.

Hardly any of them bounded from their cars. Dot said they probably had travelers' legs. Let them alone, she said, and get away from the window.

I watched as it hit them. The aromatic force of thousands of orange trees in bloom turned their faces blank. They stood in the grass, trying to adjust to the sweetness of the air. They pulled it in by the lungful. It was like a pot of marmalade burning on the stove. One of Dad's cousins would come walking out of the dark green wall of trees behind the fruit stand, carrying a crate of oranges. One lady began clapping with excitement when she saw it, like she was at a performance.

The eighty acres of groves behind the fruit stand at Hopewell had been in Dad's family since 1902. Uncle Roy was in charge of the operation, being the eldest, but his sons worked alongside him in the groves that one day would be passed on to them. Dad and Aunt Anne owned their father's thirteen acres at Hopewell. Uncle Roy took care of the trees and Dot took care of Uncle Roy, and for three glorious months of the year, she ran the fruit stand.

I spent more time at the fruit stand that winter than I ever had. A vague memory suggests that my mother or father dropped me off there a lot.

It was the first season Dot entrusted me to operate the fruit washer. It was a noisy contraption with a conveyor belt, like a car wash for oranges. The dirty oranges moved, hopped, and bounced like nervous victims toward their cleaning. The washer was a limb-sucking industrial accident waiting to happen. According to state law, no one under sixteen was supposed to operate the machine, but Aunt Dot had the final word. If you were a child who had shown responsibility and did not cuss or act the fool, you got to work the fruit washer. "Tie your hair back and keep your sleeves away from the feeder," she said.

Dot left the fruit stand at 11:30 every day to get lunch ready for Uncle Roy and the field hands. She hauled butt down the dirt road in a cloud of dust, ran in the house, put on her apron, took the butter out to soften, and started pulling the casseroles out of the fridge that she'd made at five that morning. Her kitchen was a work of art. She'd painted it herself, red and white, an homage to the strawberry. At noon sharp, she rang the heavy dinner bell on the back steps of the kitchen, and the men appeared from the groves. She heaped their plates with pork chops, string beans, corn casserole, and biscuits.

Uncle Roy thanked the Lord for this nourishment to their bodies and for dying on the cross on their behalf. They dug in while Dot speed cleaned and got the sink ready for washing dishes. The uncles moved to softer chairs, where their heads dropped and their mouths fell open, carried off by Paul Harvey's voice on the radio. A half hour later they woke like startled babies and left by the back door to return to the groves. Dot's car was already on the dirt road back to the fruit stand, kicking up dust as she put on her lipstick in the rearview mirror.

"Tell me what I missed," she said when she got back.

She knew how to deal with the Yankees. She invited them out back to show how she made her own orange blossom honey from the beehives we kept in the groves. The white boxes were stacked six high and stuck together from the output of five hundred bees. Dot would then sell the honey out of her front room from a wooden keg with a spigot.

The most famous customer to visit the fruit stand was Lucille Ball, who arrived in disguise, with a scarf over her hair and big sunglasses. She touched the various crates and smelled the different oranges, holding them up to the nose of her male friend. Aunt Dot didn't recognize her. No one did, until the very end, when a dog recognized the familiar voice and jumped in Lucy's convertible. Everyone helped get the dog out, and Lucy left with a half bushel of Hull oranges in the back seat.

When the customers drove off, sometimes Dot came out and watched them as they disappeared down the road.

DOT DIDN'T need my services all day. I rode horses with my cousins through the groves behind the fruit stand. Technically, we were second cousins; our fathers were the actual cousins who'd all grown up together. Callie was Dwight's age, a raspy-voiced blond girl who tore through the sand on her pony, Flag. Frances was my age and liked reenacting beauty pageants and religious experiences in the playhouse in Dot's backyard. She played the preacher and I played the sinner who was supposed to accept Jesus Christ as my savior. I was never able to deliver the fervor she needed, and she was hungry for fervor. Frances had thick black hair and round violet-blue eyes, and even as a child, her charisma was fierce. Her eyes bored through me as she waited for my answer.

Okay, okay, I'll take him as God's only begotten son and my savior. Frances slumped, like a rag doll, losing all dramatic tension. I never tired of Frances, but, Jesus, he was boring. I told Frances I had been saved enough for that day.

I'd stand at the edge of the trees and watch for cars

on State Road 60. When one appeared, I tried to memorize it, making note of the color and model in case I ever needed to be a witness in a trial. I liked seeing the different license plates and guessing where the people were going. I watched for Panky Snow, the lady reporter for the *Plant City Courier*, who drove a wood-sided Rambler. I saw my father with his filthy Ford and his restlessness, his arm hanging from the open window and the hot wind making his face greasy.

YANKEES OFTEN got stuck when they drove into the groves to help themselves to the fruit. They usually bogged down in the sandy rows driving out. A picker would have to climb down from his ladder to politely offer assistance. Even the lowly laborers who earned ten dollars a day were expected to follow the directives set forth by Florida Citrus Mutual: each of us was an ambassador of sunshine. We were all in this together, Citrus Mutual said.

Dot was in the back stocking honey when a man came into the fruit stand asking for the owner. He drove a white Plymouth with Pennsylvania tags. When Dot came out, he introduced himself and said he was interested in buying one of her hand-painted signs on the highway. Confusion gathered in Dot's eyes. She never made sport of the Yankees. She came around the counter to get closer to the man. "Sugar," she said, lowering her voice, "it's the fruit that's for sale."

The man shifted his weight. He explained that he worked at an art gallery in Philadelphia. He told her about the different kinds of art he collected, native folk painters and Winslow Homer and on and on, Dot growing more restless by the second. Her eyes kept wandering to the bin of tangelos that needed restocking. Finally, she cracked her red drugstore smile and said, "Honey, if the signs mean that much to you, help yourself. There's more out back." The rest of the day she recounted the story to Uncle Roy, a friend from Sunday School, a friend from art club, at least two cousins, and then whatever relative who wandered into the fruit stand. "Don't they just *tickle* you?" she asked.

The child Yankees were the ones I felt sorry for. Their parents had slathered white stuff on the tops of their ears. They reeked of camphoric sunburn ointments. Some wore hats and sunglasses. I had never seen children in sunglasses. They looked like small blind adults.

IT WASN'T just our fruit stand; the entire geography of Central Florida was waiting for the tourists. The roadside vendors had taken up their positions, tent poles dug in and World War II parachutes strung over them. The flat horizon was alight with cooking fires tended by old men stirring vats of boiled peanuts with broom handles. The carnival danced at the corner of your eye if you were paying attention.

My father took me around to see some of these places. Maybe he longed for the old days when I was his six-year-old sidekick bouncing through the groves in his Ford.

WE DROVE out Highway 60 toward the county line, where the land opened up even more and the gravel flew up into our car. We stopped at one place that was nothing more than a card table, a box of tangerines, and peanuts boiling in a vat of salty water. Dad made a show out of looking over the anemic tangerines before saying he believed he'd take a dollar's worth of the boiled peanuts. The hot paper bag sat on the seat between us as we rode home, digging in by the fistful and pitching the wet shells out the window. When we got back to our fruit stand, it seemed like a cathedral.

It was a good feeling to know that we were more than a card table on the side of the road. We had a big house and the best fruit stand, and maybe everything would work out.

CHAPTER 13

Tangelos, tangerines, Thompson grapefruit, Duncan grapefruit, ruby reds, Ambersweets, Hamlins, and Valencias. My mother was still lousy on her citrus, but she knew two important things that spring: Valencia season had just started, the most grueling three months of the year, and we lived ten blocks from Tony Mike's.

Tony Mike's was a windowless bar and package store. The actual Tony Mike was a Lebanese immigrant and long-time Plant City resident. The town gossip was that when he tried to donate money for the new building at the hospital, the Baptists who sat on the board rejected his check because of the taint of liquor money. All that soapboxing made some of the Baptists so thirsty they called Tony Mike at the store and asked if he wouldn't mind bringing a bottle around to the rear door for pickup. That's how the back door at Tony Mike's became known as the First Baptist Entrance.

My father had started dropping in at Tony Mike's more frequently than anyone knew. One morning he stopped there while taking my brother to kindergarten. It was 7:45 a.m.

Dad left Dwight in the car in the parking lot and came out of Tony Mike's with a brown paper bag. He got in the car and unscrewed the cap on the bottle, his hands shaking. He turned to Dwight: "Son, don't you ever take a taste of liquor."

Tony Mike's seemed to chew at my mother. It was too close for comfort, "on the way home" from just about everything. If my father was late for dinner, her first thought was Tony Mike's. My brother and I were hanging around the kitchen one night as she made dinner, my father still not home, and suddenly she remembered she needed milk. We piled in the car to go to the store, but the store was the other way. My mother slowed to a glide in front of Tony Mike's. It was a lazy feeling except for my mother's eyes, robotic and processing every inch of the asphalt parking lot. No sign of my father's car. She pulled a U-turn and said she could use coffee cream instead of milk. We wouldn't be stopping for milk after all.

THE *RAT-A-TAT-TAT* sound started after we were in bed. Most nights, my mother was at the dining room table with her typewriter under the crystal chandelier. *Rat-a-tat-tat* and then a sharp bell—*ding!* It was like a mechanical lullaby that made my eyes close.

Once I came down for a glass of water and spied on her from around the corner. She had a cigarette going in a small red ashtray next to the typewriter. She used the funny round eraser with a little black broom to sweep away the eraser crumbs when she made a mistake.

The thing I wanted to know was how she learned to type

so fast. I asked her to show me how to type and where to put my fingers. But I never asked her *what* she was typing.

I found out years later when going through old musty bound copies of the *Plant City Courier* in the local historical society. That terrible year in Plant City, my mother wrote a column for the newspaper. The topic was modern mother-hood. She wrote in the persona of a wife and mother navigating the demands of New Year's resolutions, children's birthday parties, and appointments at the beauty salon. The writing was blithe and witty, and none of it true.

I CAME home from school and my father's car was in the drive-way. He was never home at three o'clock. He didn't answer when I called out, so I went upstairs. It was all bright after-noon sunlight except for my parents' bedroom. I looked into the pitch-black darkness and smelled the familiar reek of Dad's clothes—cigarettes and oranges. He must have had the flu.

When he came down later, my mother served him a spe-cial dinner. It looked like the same kind of mush you fed a baby bird with an eyedropper. Bits of torn-up white bread floated in a bowl of warm milk, with a soft-boiled egg on top. My father saw me eyeing the concoction, which, according to him, was a dish called Wild Cat.

"You've never heard of Wild Cat before?" he asked, turn-ing it back on me like I was the one living in a fog of igno-rance. He spooned up some more and went back to bed.

ON A Saturday in May, my father said we had to check an orange grove. It was likely a Valencia grove because the school year was almost over and the Valencia orange came later than the others. Dwight and I had to go with him, he said. I didn't want to go to the grove at all. His car was dirty and his AC was broken and blowing dust and bugs everywhere. It stank of fertilizer.

Dwight was in back, his blond hair whipping back in a car traveling too fast on a narrow road. I was in the front, gauging the distance to the irrigation ditches on either side.

The grove was empty when we got there. I looked down every row to see if there were any trucks or workers. No trucks, no workers, just heat and a thousand buzzing cicadas, getting louder by the minute. You couldn't see them. They were inside the orange trees.

Normally my father got out of the car to inspect the fruit, but this time he just drove through the grid of shadows, taking the turns too sharply before heading up another row. The whip antenna thrashed the tree branches, snapping fruit off the stem. Leaves flew through the air.

"Dad!" I said, loud enough to startle him.

He stopped the car in the middle of the row. He cut the engine and sat there for a second. Then he reached across the front seat and opened the glove compartment, the one we were never meant to open. Inside, his gun was waiting there.

He brought the gun out and held it in his lap. He opened the chamber and shut it.

"Are there bad men?" Dwight asked, because my father had told us that the gun was for snakes and bad men. Dwight began to cry, louder.

"No, son," my father said.

He put the gun down on the dashboard. He grabbed the

steering wheel with both hands. His body caved in on itself. He heaved, and laid his head against the steering wheel.

He pushed the gun to the corner of the windshield, as far away from him as possible. With the other hand, he opened his door and got sick.

Dwight was crying. The image sticks with me still. The dirty yellow Ford, sitting in the middle of a magnificent grove of Valencias, the trees so much taller than the three passengers inside the car. A breeze of raw honey and burned marmalade moved through the grove, trapping us all in the sweetness.

My father climbed back into the car. He had brushed most of the vomit off his pants with a handkerchief. We drove home.

CHAPTER 14

The following Monday, I was sitting at my desk in Mrs. Mackey's classroom, making elaborate loops with my pencil during cursive writing, when my mother appeared at the door. Any time a parent showed up it usually was not good. One of us was about to get culled from the herd. This time it was me. I looked straight ahead and pretended it wasn't, until Mrs. Mackey told me to gather my things. The pencils and coins rattled inside my cigar box as I walked out of the classroom.

My mother had my school records. I didn't understand what was happening. The school year was over in two weeks. We got to the parking lot and I saw her car, packed for an extended trip. Piled on top of our suitcases in the back seat were our clothes, still on their hangers. Dwight was also back there, sitting placidly amid the contents of our closets, drinking a grape soda and showing no signs of distress. I saw the silver frame of Mom's favorite *Don Quixote* print. Even before she said anything, the connective wires had started to spark in my mind.

In the car, she gave a vague explanation that Dad's illness was not getting better, so we were going to stay at her mother's house in St. Petersburg. She tried to make it sound like an event that was a long time coming, looking over at me for reaction, but I was without words for once. We'd never spoken about my father's "illness."

The car sagged in the desperate way that all vehicles do when overloaded. Before coming to pick me up, she'd gone to the bank to empty her savings account. The bank teller gave her a hard time about making a transaction without my father's signature. When Mom said the account was in her name and did not require my father's signature, the teller made a big show of calling over the manager. My mother prevailed, all for a lousy four hundred dollars.

The envelope of cash was thin, sealed shut with the hateful spittle of the bank teller who got in a last dig as she handed over the money: "Here you are. Bless your heart."

Every few minutes on the way to St. Petersburg, my mother checked her wristwatch as if we were in a rush. She wanted to be far down the road before my father got home from work. You could see the hesitation in her fitful driving, with a light foot on the gas pedal, willing herself to keep going. I was in my own weakened state and getting weaker by the minute. It appeared we would not be returning. Suddenly it was imperative for me to know if my mother remembered my Girl Scout sash.

"Did you?" I asked with prosecutorial zeal. I had worked hard for those badges.

She had forgotten the sash.

We stopped at a traffic light downtown in front of Kirby's Bakery. The ladies in hairnets were laughing behind the counter, sliding in trays of crème horns and Chinese chews, going on about their lives. I blinked a few times to keep the tears away, trying to focus on the scene inside Kirby's, when I felt my mother reaching for me with tenderness. "No," I said, rearing so far back into the metal car door that the handle jammed into my ribs.

The light turned green, but we sat there without moving. My mother had her foot on the brake.

"Mom! Earth to Mom," I said.

Finally, she remembered to press the accelerator. Plant City slid by. We bypassed the road to our house, taking a different route. Not even one last look. On my dresser in my bedroom was my horse collection. I wondered who would get the horses.

We drove west into the glare. The Spanish moss disappeared from the trees and the sun grew brighter. Pastures gave way to gas stations that gave way to Arthur Treacher's Fish & Chips. Then we reached the interstate. It was brand new, flying above east Tampa. The buildings down below sparkled with quartz except for one part lined with slums. You could see little wooden shacks with dirt yards and chickens pecking around in the dirt and laundry strung across sagging porches and the sun beating down with all its might on the shacks.

Cars shot past us on the interstate. I thought I saw Panky Snow, the reporter lady who used to stop at the fruit stand with a pencil in her teased hair, but it was someone else in a green Rambler station wagon.

Soon, the air turned salty. Water was everywhere, blue and lapping at the pilings of a long bridge that carried us into St. Petersburg. The clouds in the sky were as white as cake frosting. At the water's edge were twisted mangroves, low to the ground. There was not a single orange tree in sight, no shade whatsoever except for the slim shadow of a seagull as it passed overhead. I put up my hand to shield my eyes.

Just as we were cresting the bridge and I was secretly scanning the water for dolphins, my mother said, "Oh, God."

On the far side, she pulled off onto the shoulder. Traffic zoomed by. The parking spot was less than ideal. The drivers here liked to tow boats and campers and other wide, swaying appendages, but Mom was determined to get back to the trunk. She kept her eyes on the side mirror, waiting for a break in the Indy 500, and when her grip on the door handle tightened, it was obvious she was going for it. "Stay in the car," she said.

My mother wasn't cautious, but she wasn't reckless. To watch her shimmying sideways along the side of the car was terrifying. The velocity of the traffic lifted up her blouse. Her hair was plastered against her face. She eased back to the trunk, brave and hell-bent.

This should have given me comfort; instead, foreboding swept through the pit of my stomach. At that moment, my mother was the remaining parent. She was all we had.

Somehow, she made it to the trunk. The lid went up and we lost sight of her. Dwight asked for a piece of Bazooka gum and I said I was out. "Liar," he said. "Please?" I gave him one.

There was nothing to do but look at the water. A chop had picked up and the sky had darkened. A seagull parked itself in the wind at three o'clock, hovering the same way a vulture would hover, agile and calculating. The trunk slammed shut. My mother made her way back, scooting sideways to avoid getting creamed by the outside lane of traffic as she slid back into the car. Windblown and glistening with sweat, she opened the metal document box. I saw my birth certificate go by with the small ink footprint as she riffled through the papers. When she found her teaching certificate, she put it in her purse. That little piece of paper she risked her life for was the only way she could find a teaching job in St. Petersburg.

WE ARRIVED at my grandmother's house. Not Gigi but my other grandmother, Olive Lee Desmond, or Damie, pronounced "Dah-MEE"—my attempt at "grandma" when I was eighteen months old. The name stuck. Her front yard was lined with two-story-high palm trees, tall as skyscrapers.

Until my mother opened her car door, nothing was final. She stared at the brown cement house, suspended between our old life and new life. The sun bore down on the Cutlass. The goldfish in the bowl was starting to cook. Then she did it. She yanked up her door handle and was out of the car.

"Take these," she said, thrusting her Clairol Kindness hot rollers at me. She scooped up an armful of clothes from the back seat and disappeared. She left me holding the little briefcase handle of the box of hair curlers. I couldn't take another step. Once she was inside the house, I sat down in the driveway and sobbed.

CHAPTER 15

The first week at Damie's house I wet the bed again. I tried to hide it by staying in the piss-soaked sheets until morning, but my mother got up in the middle of the night to check the sheets. She had to turn on the overhead light to do it, and it woke my grandmother up. I was sharing her bedroom. "Mama, I'm sorry," my mother said to her. It happened every few nights. I was terrified my grandmother was going to kick us out. Instead she bought me a red transistor radio like the one she had under her pillow at night. I set my channel to her channel and we listened to music in the dark.

My mother waited to hear back from the county about a teaching job in St. Pete, circling help wanted ads in the paper, just in case. After two weeks, she finally got her phone call, but it wasn't the county. It was her principal from down in Sebring saying he heard she was looking for a job. Sebring was the last place my mother wanted to go, but we had no choice. My grandmother waved goodbye from her front yard. One arm was clasped behind her back, like a navy admiral.

"Arrivederci, dahling," she said, in her elusive show of emotion. "Until we meet again."

WE RETURNED to Sebring with an air of defeat, taking a fleabag apartment downtown, a mile from where we'd lived in that sparkling new subdivision by the lake when I was in first grade. I didn't know anyone whose parents had broken up.

Mom cleaned the crummy wood frame duplex from top to bottom, fully furnished with dingy couches and yellowed mattresses, no air-conditioning. The other half was rented by a neighbor with cats. And fleas. Every Saturday we set off a flea bomb canister. Mom covered up the dishes and silverware to keep the poison off. Dwight and I went around closing all the windows. When Mom set off the aerosol canister, we hauled ass out the back door carrying our laundry baskets. We killed the next four hours at the laundromat, while the death spray settled on our fleas and roaches at home.

Our parking space was in a sandy alley where the car often bogged down. My mother tried to rock the heavy Cutlass out, putting it in drive and gently pressing the accelerator to go forward a few inches, then throwing the gear in reverse and accelerating again, until we finally surged free. She developed a pathological fear of our car breaking down. The tiniest tick, the slightest noise, and she threw her hand up like a sniper who'd just heard a twig break, ordering us to be silent. We weren't allowed to talk until she was satisfied the sound was just a pebble flying up into the wheel well. The idea of not being able to get to work terrified her. Her paycheck came every two weeks and never soon enough.

Weekends were hard. Saturday was flea bomb day. On

Sunday, the entire town was shut down, stores were closed. We didn't go to church, like everyone else, but my mother kept up the tradition of Sunday noon dinner. She cooked a pot roast for us, the only time all week we could afford meat. Then she'd take a nap. The town was quiet in the blast heat of summer after the churches emptied out. Dwight and I walked down to City Pier with fishing lines and hooks. We didn't have fishing poles, but I could ball up white bread and hook it, then drop it off the pier and wait. I gave the crusts to Dwight. They didn't wrap around the hook very well, so the fish took his offering and swam away. Sometimes I caught a bream. We'd carry the twitching fish in a plastic pail back to our mother, who would give it to the cats in the alley.

My mother's teacher posse rallied around her, bringing Dwight and me clothes that their kids had outgrown. They showed up at our house after the school day ended with pots and pans. They invited us to their two-parent homes for dinner. When one of them visited us for the first time, Mom spread her arms wide like a game show host and said, "Welcome to modern poverty."

SHE TRIED to keep life normal by volunteering as an assistant Brownie troop leader. At one of the Brownie meetings, a mother brought in a box of grocery store cupcakes. They were the good kind, with the Crisco frosting that put a two-day coat of Turtle Wax on the roof of your mouth. We were supposed to take one. Alone at the table with the open box of cupcakes, I grabbed an extra and put it inside paper towels. A girl saw me and yelled, "SHE took TWO!" The troop leader and my mother were outside having a cigarette and the other girls weren't that interested in the crime stopper's announcement, but she'd put me in the display case of shame. Food wasn't scarce at home; I hoarded treats. Glazed, frosted, cream-filled, Little Debbies, raspberry Zingers, elephant ears at the bakery, anything we couldn't afford.

After Thanksgiving, I came down with a terrible ear infection. It felt like someone had taken a hammer to one side of my head and I was burning up with fever. My mother couldn't afford to take off a day from teaching, so she gave me baby aspirin, then left for school with Dwight. I stayed at home by myself all day, hallucinating eerie figures on the bedroom wall. My mother called every hour from the teachers' lounge to check on me. I was in tears, disoriented and scared. But she had to return to her classroom.

DWIGHT NEVER veered from his sweet nature, unperturbed by our freefall. His outlook remained sunny. His musings delighted my mother. "I know how stars are made," he said. "When the sun goes down, it collapses and the broken parts are stars."

MY MOTHER had brought us here and I hated it. My tenth birthday was that June. She scraped up eight dollars for a birthday gift by putting two dollars a week on store layaway. She knew I didn't like wearing other girls' castoff clothes. On my birthday, she excitedly presented her gift—a red, white, and blue matching outfit of flared jeans and an American flag shirt.

I saw my opportunity: "I don't like it."

Her shoulders fell. "What kind of child have I raised?" she said. She wasn't asking me; she was asking herself, which was ten times worse.

I slunk out of the room.

Soon after that, she got the call she'd been hoping for, a teaching position in St. Petersburg at an elementary school. After a year in Sebring, we headed back to my grandmother's house in St. Pete. Dwight and I did a little jig.

Leaving Sebring the second time, we barely made it out. Our car was so loaded down with our belongings it wouldn't budge from the sand behind our house. My mother rocked us back and forth, back and forth, and finally just floored it, prying us loose from that shit year in Sebring. I didn't so much as turn my head.

CHAPTER 16

The only people in St. Petersburg were old people. They rested on bus benches or clickety-clacked down the sidewalk on canes and walkers. I saw at least two with gauze bandages over an eye. They wore little clip-on sunshades that fit over their prescription glasses. We stopped for a red light. Sitting at the bus stop was a lady who had to be eighty years old and she was wearing a Howard Johnson's waitress uniform.

There was so much I would soon learn about St. Pete. That it was known as God's Waiting Room. That it was not just a haven for retirees, but a particular kind of retiree—from Ohio, Wisconsin, Michigan, and Illinois. The bold East Coast retirees lived in Miami in turquoise houses. The Midwesterners came to St. Pete and ate creamed corn. My grandmother from Brooklyn didn't really belong in a city that had only one Jewish deli, a place called Wolfie's, where she went once a week for challah bread and beef tongue. Only she didn't just go to Wolfie's, she said she "schlepped" there.

She was standing in her front yard to greet us as we pulled in. I searched her face, looking for any sign that she might be mad at us for coming back. Instead, she clasped her hands as if it were the happiest day of her life and exclaimed, "Hello, dahling!"

Here cement block houses were painted in Necco Wafer colors. Pale pink and seafoam green and chalky yellow, all with white barrel tile roofs that looked like cake frosting against the blue sky. Most of the houses had a grapefruit or tangerine tree in the yard that the people had encircled in decorative stones. Damie's house was chocolate colored, with a small ceramic statue of St. Francis of Assisi in the yard.

Dwight and I rushed over to St. Francis in the grass. We'd never seen a white lawn ornament wearing rags. St. Francis had on a brown sack cinched by a piece of rope, the ceramic paint so lifelike you saw fibers fraying on the rope. He didn't seem the least bit put out by his situation. Jesus always had a poor-me look, not one to pass up a chance to remind you of everything he'd done for you. All St. Francis had was a bird sitting on his shoulder.

Damie's yard had big brambles of honeysuckle and gardenia shrubs underneath her bedroom windows because she'd always wanted to wake up to fragrance, to maximize waft. Her yard on a big corner lot was a series of ecosystems determined by how far she could stretch the hose. The side yard was a sub-Sahara full of lizards. She tried to go with it, putting in cactus and aloe plants, a torture pit for the barefooted. Everything else was a spongy green carpet of St. Augustine grass, bouncy as a moonwalk with tall queen palm trees swaying overhead. Up and down the block was silent and still. Not a single bike was thrown down in the grass.

Dwight hollered for me to come to the backyard. I went around the corner of my grandmother's house and stopped.

A huge assortment of bras, girdles, and panties were

hanging on the clothesline, the bras so large in size they looked like those slings the coast guard dropped down from a helicopter to perform a water rescue. There was no fence or privacy shrubs, just a huge RV parked in the neighbor's yard with a message painted on the back:

THERE GO THE WENKS
HELEN AND FRANK.

My mother cleaned for two solid days. Rubber gloves, sleeveless blouse, and pots of coffee. She found oyster crackers under seat cushions and spoons that had hardened to the floor after going overboard as Damie ate New England clam chowder on the couch. Mom was at the kitchen counter scrubbing teriyaki stains out of the grout with a toothbrush when my grandmother paused to watch.

"That's Victoria," Damie said with bemused detachment. "She was that way when she was thirteen." Book in hand, she adjourned outside to her glider swing.

Once the house was clean we could start our lives fresh. My brother had trouble understanding where my father was. Mom thought it would help if we called my brother by a different name. Lose the "Dwight"—an old Hull family name swaddled in a hundred years of Hopewell moss—and maybe it would lessen the shadow of my father's absence. All four of us sat in Damie's living room trying to think of a new name for my brother. If he was bothered by having seven years of his identity snatched away, he didn't show it.

"Carlos!" he shouted, like a *Jeopardy!* contestant. Damie suggested J.D., short for James Dwight, his legal name. In the end we decided on Jim. My mother took him to the five-dollar-an-hour county services family therapist to make sure he was okay with the change.

Dwight being Dwight, he slid happily into Jim. After a week, we forgot he was ever Dwight.

My mother left my name alone, but I wanted to become someone new, too. Not the girl in Sebring who wore donated clothes to school and asked Theresa Barnes for bites of her Lebanon bologna sandwich. In St. Pete, I could be anyone I wanted to be.

Living in the clutter and crap of Damie's house was hard for my mother. Not only was her marriage in shreds, she also woke up to tribal masks, hookah pipes, Chinese scrolls, Bombay wicker fans, and several hundred used paperbacks with moth wings between the pages. I liked being back in the twin bed in my grandmother's room with a transistor radio under my pillow. We still listened to music in the dark. Damie would point out which Beatle was playing a certain guitar part in "Hey Jude." I didn't care for the Beatles. But we agreed on the Chi-Lites and the Main Ingredient, and we wouldn't close our eyes until "Everybody Plays the Fool" came on.

Mom's brother, Uncle Rod, had also taken up residence in my grandmother's house. Damie said he was drying out and trying to get back on his feet. Uncle Rod was moody. He had the same green-gray marble eyes as my mother, only his were like two-way mirrors you couldn't see behind. He was deeply tanned from afternoons at Pass-a-Grille Beach and riding in his car, a 1962 Thunderbird convertible. It was the only thing of value that he owned. He polished it and buffed it with a chamois; the second he got home from the beach he vacuumed the floor mats.

Uncle Rod made it seem like we weren't as broke as we were, because of his job at Moock's Tavern. Moock's was where all the ballplayers who came to St. Pete for spring training got drunk at night. Uncle Rod was the overnight security guard. He had to deal with a lot of puking in the bushes and screwing in cars. Once the place emptied out, he sat in a booth and read his AA books, drinking club soda.

I was in the kitchen the next morning when he came home bearing steaks or chops or whatever else he'd lifted from the walk-in cooler at Moock's. He put his gun on top of the fridge and I turned on the burner. He then demonstrated how to properly cook a rare steak. A very hot pan was the secret. He called it the ex-con breakfast. Around 9 a.m. he said good night and went to bed. My brother came into the kitchen with his sheepdog hair in his eyes and no shirt, wondering if Uncle Rod had brought home the giant container of milk with the suction hose and nozzle. He said he could never drink milk again unless it was through a hose.

My mother was gone teaching summer school all day. At night she went to the library to study for the GRE so she could earn more as a teacher with a master's degree. That left my grandmother to provide adult supervision. She didn't emerge from her bedroom until nearly eleven in the morning. Twice a week, around eight in the morning, long before Damie was up, the Hood's Dairy man pulled up in his white truck and delivered the order she had left for him on the porch on a slip of paper with boxes to check. Jim and I made the most of our freedom. We retrieved the slip of paper from the milk crate. All you had to do was check the box and the guy brought it the next morning. We ordered sherbet, chocolate milk, and whatever else looked good. We took the sherbet to the vacant lot next door, bringing two spoons from the kitchen drawer, and ate it in the heat. Regular sherbet never tasted as good as the scammed product.

If Damie noticed the dairy bill, she didn't say so. It was hard to know what she thought about bills or anything else; she avoided direct statements, and even if she offered a negative opinion, it didn't sound negative because she spoke in full sonnets in her faux aristocratic accent from her girlhood training. She read James Michener in bed, from midnight to two, her massive breasts falling sideways out of her nightgown as she turned the pages of *Tales of the South Pacific*. There was late-night music playing on the transistor radio she kept under her pillow. If she wanted to hear a song, she put in her dentures and called the request line at WLCY, telling the overnight deejay that George Harrison had finally come into his own on *Abbey Road*.

Her day began at brunch with cheese toast or challah bread from the Jewish deli, orange marmalade, cottage cheese, prune juice, Maxwell House, and the *St. Petersburg Times* spread out on the yellow dinette table in the kitchen. After putting her dishes in the sink, she carried the paper to the couch and resumed her reading. She kept a notepad nearby. This is where her letters-to-the-editor ideas started to germinate. She believed that the newspaper was the last recourse for the elderly. For two weeks she called the power company to report a broken streetlight on our corner, and when they ignored her requests for service, she whipped out her floral stationery and decried the callousness of the public utilities in a letter to the editor.

"It is just as if we were transported in a time machine back to the 18th century of Sam Johnson's London, where, in the darkness of night, robbers and highwaymen lurked around corners to attack and plunder."

Around 2 p.m. she dressed to go out for the afternoon. I sat on my bed and watched the process. Her nakedness only scared me at first. She came out of the shower, dusted her naked body with lily of the valley powder, then swung her "bossies," as she called them, into her gargantuan bra with four hooks in back. That's how much closure she required to contain the heft in front. Her breasts were straight out of the *National Geographic*, pulled down by so much gravity her nipples nearly touched her belly button. She had the hugest boobs but the skinniest legs and arms. I had just started wearing a training bra.

The top of her dresser was a vast sea of crap, and she had to pick through the perfume bottles and vats of Noxzema to find the right set of costume pearls. She wore white Ban-Lon knit dresses with green polka dots, gartered stockings, and white Hush Puppies sandals.

"So long, dahlings," she said as she left the house, holding a Japanese parasol over her head to shield herself from the sun. Jim sat in the dry lawn near the street, drawing a fantasia of hypnotic swirls in the dirt. My grandmother praised his work and cited a Japanese emperor famous for his bonsai collection. Sometimes I walked with her to the bus stop, listening to her sing Tony Bennett's "Stranger in Paradise," and watched her step on the bus and disappear.

It would be dark when she returned home with some newly purchased trinkets. A straw doll from the Philippines, tribal drums from Nepal. Where she found such treasures, I had no idea.

The weird thing about her house, given that she didn't

drive or own a car, was that it had two double garages. To make an extra buck, she rented the second garage out to ball players who came down for spring training. A pair of St. Louis Cardinals had their Thunderbirds stashed inside the bays. One was a turquoise convertible with big shark fins and red taillights, a shiny beauty. I used to slide in behind the wheel in the darkened garage and pretend to drive. The seats smelled like Old Spice and the floor mats glittered with beach sand. It was a mystery to me how guys from the Cardinals and the Yankees got wind of the old lady with two big garages who lived a mile from Miller Huggins Field. They were always coming and going, leaving their rent checks shoved between the jalousie windows of her front door.

Between summer school and evening classes for her master's degree, my mother was mostly gone. She left while Jim and I were still asleep, came home briefly in the late afternoon, and then left again.

I imagined her in summer school teaching basic English to delinquents, truants, smokers, and tramps, all with cystic acne and unwashed hair. Someone had to do it and my mother needed the money, so off to work she went. Then I learned she had been assigned to a normal middle school and was spending her summer with normal kids my age. Inside, a tiny switchblade opened.

I SPENT many hours running a scam and got my brother to join me. We took an old empty Folgers can, wrapped it in paper, cut a slit in the plastic top, and went door-to-door in the neighborhood with a made-up story that we were collecting money for a school trip. Our customers were old people on guard against scammers, especially solicitors selling dance lessons from the Arthur Murray Dance Studio. Every week the paper ran a story about some lady whose bank account was drained by an Arthur Murray dance instructor. Luckily, we were children, and 95 percent of them opened their screen doors to us. The coins bounced in the can as we walked to the nearby convenience store, where we counted our loot and blew it on Nutty Buddies and Lemonheads.

Some days, we made our rounds with David, a new kid across the street. He was a year older than me. He had square shoulders and polite Southern manners he brought down from Georgia. He was the sort of boy that made old people dig for quarters. He lacked natural instinct, though, and he refused to be the one holding the coffee can.

"Daddy would whup my ass or take away football," David said. The Miami Dolphins were the focus of his life. Almost every day he wore an aquamarine Dolphins jersey with NO. 12 and GRIESE on the back. In my grandmother's front yard, he taught me how to throw a spiral like his idol. One day we lost control of the football and sent it through Damie's window. David's reaction impressed me. Instead of running home, he waited for my grandmother to come outside and chew us out. Instead, she shrugged. "Que será, será," she said and called a glass company.

My brother, Jim, was still a walking calamity, despite a new name. Somehow, we got hold of a boomerang. David and I convinced my brother to give it a test throw. We watched the boomerang swoop past the palm trees in Damie's front yard and curve back straight at Jim's forehead. He got four stitches at St. Anthony's Hospital. After a fierce afternoon rain, we were tossing a baseball around and watched helplessly as the ball rolled into the street and got sucked into the torrent of rainwater headed toward an open sewer grate. We wanted the ball back, so naturally, we put Jim into service. David took one of his ankles and I took the other, and we lowered him into the churning sewer. Our hands kept slipping on his wet skin as the current pulled at my brother.

"You see anything?" David hollered. We hauled my brother back up. Jim was drenched and coughing and wished he could go back down for another try.

OTHER GIRLS had started having crushes on boys. The only boys I cared about were my brother and Michael Jackson. I turned my bedroom wall into a Jackson 5 collage of epic proportions. It was all fitted turquoise vests and patent leather half boots. My seventy-year-old roommate didn't mind in the least. Damie was in love with the Jackson 5 too. We watched them on *The Ed Sullivan Show* with bowls of orange sherbet in our laps. Wherever she went on her mysterious afternoon travels, she brought home copies of *Right On!* and *Tiger Beat* that featured the five brothers.

"Jermaine is dahling," she said. By then I knew she wasn't trying to cozy up to me. She was sincerely nutty and a genuine J-5 fan.

When WLCY announced that the Jackson 5's second US tour would stop in Tampa, I knew it was a long shot financially. But my grandmother operated on an economic principle known as "chicken today, feathers tomorrow," which meant that the money she was supposed to give Florida Power went to a pair of Jackson 5 tickets.

We took a bus from St. Petersburg across the bridge to

Tampa. I wore bell bottoms and a knockoff Nik-Nik shirt, the same kind Michael wore under his vests. My grandmother carried a wicker handbag. All I'd ever seen of Curtis Hixon Hall were the televised wrestling matches with Dusty Rhodes and Terry Funk doing half nelsons on each other and gushing fake blood. Now I was standing on the smooth pavilion about to see the Jackson 5. My granny and I joined the flow of afros and shags and feathered bangs, all of us moving toward the frigid blast of air-conditioning blowing from the entrance.

It was my first concert. I expected to enter a magical cave, dark and loud and nobody able to see each other. Instead, I walked into a harshly lit school assembly. And that stage! It was a puny home-carpentered piece of junk. We all stood around under bright lights that revealed the cheapness of our suede vests.

The ticket said the show started at 7 p.m. At 7, the stage was still empty. I kept asking my grandmother for the time. "Cool it," she said. Concerts often started a few minutes late, she explained. But when others started chanting, I did, too. We demanded not another moment go by without the Jacksons. "We want the Jacksons. We want the Jacksons. The Jackson 5 now."

God himself must have pulled the master switch killing the lights. It happened so fast and so totally I reached out for my grandmother. "I'm here, dahling," she said, her white Keds iridescent in the dark. A spotlight shone on the stage, revealing the five brothers. My grandmother in her plastic pearls watched us all lose our minds.

How to describe the opening of "I Want You Back"? The fingers flying down the piano keys, the rhythm guitar, the cymbals, the start of something. The Jackson 5 danced, spun, dipped, and busted moves in their zippered ankle boots until finally the littlest brother stepped to the microphone. That beseeching joyous falsetto washed away all the candy blood of the wrestlers who'd faked it in this dark cavern.

all I want a buh buh buh buh
all I need a buh buh buh buh

Mom picked us up after the show in her beater car. How was it, she asked, first me and then my grandmother, who said "brilliant" and that she intended to write a letter to the Jacksons' parents congratulating them on raising five wonderful young men.

CHAPTER 17

My mother tried to get us into St. Paul's, her old Catholic school two blocks from my grandmother's house. It was ideal for us in every way, except we couldn't afford the tuition and we weren't Catholic. She went to see the principal. The nuns she knew from her days at St. Paul's were gone. Just as well. Returning to the redbrick school without knowing anyone made it easier to ask for charity. No one there knew about the days when she spent thousands of hours editing the yearbook, running the Spanish club, decorating the gym for prom, and rehearsing for debate club.

When she came home, my grandmother looked up from her paper and said how wonderful it must have been for my mother to see her alma mater! My mother kicked off her shoes, took off her clip earrings, and sat down with a long, exhausted sigh. It wasn't worth telling my grandmother what it was really like going back to St. Paul's. All she said is that most of the nuns she knew were gone.

She struck some kind of deal with Sister Bernadette. We got in. My mother still had to come up with money for school uniforms. We had to go to a special Catholic uniform supply store for my plaid skirt since normal stores didn't sell Catholic garb.

I would have to wear the plaid skirt five days a week. Normally not my style, but I didn't mind. It was the answer to my prayers, in fact. It saved me from wearing my beat-up real clothes that screamed "broken home." My mother went to pick up the new skirt from the dry cleaners. It was hard and stiff from anti-wrinkle chemicals. She set it on the car seat like a lamp shade and drove it home, where it stunk up the bedroom for a week.

If anyone asked, I said I was from Brooklyn. It was a way to start fresh and not get bogged down by the past. In case any of my fellow fifth graders pressed for details, I memorized my mother's old address in Brooklyn. "It's near Prospect Park," I said, having no idea where Prospect Park was.

I'd never seen a real live nun up close before. Sister Jeanette had big shoulders and meaty hands. She could've played defensive tackle for the Dolphins, the seams of her habit pulling to the point of busting. Sister Rosetta was short and stocky, like an older waitress at an Italian family restaurant. Sister Mary was elfin and not much taller than the sixth graders she taught.

After the last bell, the nuns flanked out across school grounds to make sure students left in an orderly fashion. Sister Rosetta positioned herself on the top step of the girls' locker room. One of the older nuns stood at the window of a second-floor classroom, like a sniper. Sister Mary, the quickest and youngest, covered the area behind the rectory and convent.

After lunch one day in Sister Mary's class, we were about to start with a prayer when she signaled for us to stop and bent down for something behind her desk. A guitar. Next thing you know, she's strapping it on and tuning the strings like Joan Baez. Within a week, we could sing, "One Bread, One Body." Sister Mary didn't mind starting over.

"Let's take it from 'Blood of the Lamb,'" she said, tapping out the beat with her black shoe. We never recited a prayer in her class again. She gambled that music would make us feel closer to God.

The school had given me a list of basic prayers to memorize. The Nicene Creed was more than two hundred words long! I didn't even know what a Nicene was. I was years behind the proficiency of my classmates, who throughout the day rattled off prayers in unison on demand. They used the same strange robotic cadence in every prayer. After a few days of standing in the middle of the robot colony with my cheat sheet, it became obvious. You didn't have to know all the words to the prayers as long as you used the same Zombie cadence.

When I blanked on the words, I repeated the lyrics in the Coke commercial.

> *I'd like to teach the world to sing*
> *In perfect harmony*
> *I'd like to buy the world a Coke*
> *And keep it company*

The only sister who took note was Sister Jeanette, the linebacker. Unfortunately, she was my homeroom teacher. Sunlight poured into her corner classroom and Cuban royal palm fronds brushed against the windows. A perfect setting except for Sister Jeanette, who walked up and down the rows of desks as we recited our prayers, a metal-edged ruler in her hands. Over her dead body would she adopt the slack practices of these 1970s nuns and their guitars or their tambourines. Sister Jeanette had an uncanny knack for rooting out fakers and malingerers. Mumblers were also a scourge, even the kid with the cleft lip who was trying his best. She put her giant pasty face inches from his and said, "Enunciate!"

Something about me bothered Sister Jeanette. The first week of school when I was brand-new at St. Paul's, she told me to pick up my feet when I walk. I told her I had blisters from my new saddle shoes. I even showed her. Steadying myself on the desk, I hoisted my foot up to let her see where the blood had come through my white sock. "Don't you have Band-Aids at home?" she asked. Maybe she knew I was on reduced tuition and free lunch.

Lesson number one: do not under any circumstances give Sister Jeanette a clean shot at outstretched fingers. She rapped the desk with her ruler, an inch from my fingers. Maybe this is how she broke in newcomers.

Later that week I talked during quiet time. One lousy sentence, and not even very loud, to the girl in front of me. Suddenly there was a big fat finger pointing at me from the front of the classroom. "Lady Jane," she said, her dead gray eyes on me. Instead of learning our names, she called each girl "Lady Jane." "Did you not hear me, Lady Jane?"

It got worse when she caught me laughing. Happiness unsettled her, mine especially. She ordered me to place my hands palms down on the desk and brought down the ruler so hard it broke the skin on the middle finger and bruised the three others.

Many of my classmates got the ruler, which lessened the humiliation of being singled out.

I WANTED to be popular, but the cost was high. Little by little, I got the picture that there was only one way to do it. I'd been strong enough to fend off Aunt Anne's cuticle kit when I was six, but I was no match for an army of fifth-grade girls. We all wore the same dark plaid skirts, but the cool girls at St. Paul's wore their plaid skirts low on their hips. They did this by rolling down the waistband. It made them saunter. I studied their technique and rolled my waistband down, too. Pretty soon we were all sauntering to the cafeteria together. My shelf life as a tomboy was expiring.

Other things were harder, like carrying my notebook in the crook of my arm. It wasn't natural to go around with your elbow bent at a 90-degree angle to carry something that weighed four ounces. It made no sense. My arm was exhausted from holding it that way and I wanted to drop it so bad, just let it rest on my hip like the guys, but no. I couldn't wait to walk home from school and carry my notebook the normal way, one-handed.

At the start of the year, a yellow VW bug had arrived in the teacher's parking lot. Out stepped Miss Mallory, the new fifth-grade student teacher. She was tall and tan, with long brown hair, bone straight and blond streaked, that fell down her back, unusual in Florida's humidity. When she came into the classroom, she smelled of woods and flowers. I thought up reasons to approach her desk as often as possible, just to breathe her in. Nuns didn't have any smell, but Miss Mallory did. It was like sandalwood incense cones.

One day I asked what kind of shampoo she used. Her tan face scrunched slightly and she paused. I took it as a good sign. Maybe she was struck by my observational skills.

"It's called Clairol Herbal Essence," she said.

When I went home, I asked my grandmother if she could please buy the same shampoo. She brought it back the next night. My own bottle! I took the bottle to the shower and stared at the green liquid in the palm of my hand. I studied the label showing a naked woman half-submerged in a pool of water, with flowers and butterflies in her long blond hair.

And then I rubbed it into my hair. My grandmother's postage stamp–sized bathroom with the blue tiles smelled like Miss Mallory.

MOM RECONNECTED with Bobbie, her friend from eighth grade at St. Paul's. They met after they both moved to St. Petersburg from Brooklyn. Bobbie was now a foul-mouthed single mother of three after her mechanic husband had dropped dead at thirty-six. She was blue-collar, the daughter of Polish immigrants, a screamer, and a wearer of muumuus. She had a million dumb Polack jokes. A stunner in high school who was now thirty-five pounds overweight, she and my mother did skits and impersonations, saving each other with laughter. Bobbie saved us kids by feeding us. At her house we could help ourselves to anything we wanted. She had wood-paneled cabinets full of potato chips and Oreos.

On Saturday afternoons, we went to Bobbie's house so she could color my mom's hair or give her a perm, and all around the table were other women from the neighborhood where Bobbie lived. It was like a beauty salon, everyone doing their hair, smoking cigarettes, and laughing. My mother was the only "professional" woman among them and the only divorced woman.

Mom and Bobbie did their best to keep five kids entertained and out of trouble on a shoestring budget. Walt Disney had opened his Disney World in Orlando the year before. I hated it before it ever opened. TV stations cut into their regular programming for live coverage. It was front-page news; it was practically a religious holiday in Florida. We couldn't afford to go.

We went to Lowry Park instead, a low-rent attraction that featured a large fenced-in "Serengeti" with roaming ill-tempered boars and rams, and for fifty cents, a guest could ride a kiddie train with a conductor through the wild animal park. Bobbie's son, Drew, and I had an idea: when the train passed by, we'd hop on without paying. The train came around the bend, passing some ceramic elves, and we jumped on with Jim. The sadistic train conductor waited until we were inside the fenced animal park to stop the train and kick us off. The boars and rams watched us warily as the train pulled away, a few walking toward us, then trotting. We were on their turf now.

We made a run for the eight-foot chain-link fence as hooved aggressors gave chase. I made it to the fence and scrambled up and so did Drew. My brother was within three feet of being gored when he finally got out, and that's when park security showed up. They hauled us into the main office and paged our mothers across the park. On the way home, Mom and Bobbie swore they were going to start looking for husbands.

CHAPTER 18

One afternoon my father called from a pay phone in New Orleans. He was in a booth with a stack of quarters. He'd been rehearsing the call for weeks. What to say, how to say it. His counselor at the dry-out facility told him the first step was the most important step, and the first step was to dial the number.

When the phone rang, I was on the floor of my bedroom with scissors and tape, cutting out pictures of the Jackson 5 from *Tiger Beat* so I could use them in the collage over my bed. The ceiling fan was blowing little scraps of *Tiger Beat* everywhere and the air conditioner unit was on full blast to help the pictures stick to the wall. I ran out to the sweltering living room to answer the phone.

On the other end of the line, a voice I hadn't heard in more than a year said my name.

"Dad?" I asked, standing barefoot on the terrazzo. It had to be. The deep alto, the courteousness that was slightly formal, slightly wrecked, and Southern in a way that only Central Florida citrus-growing, educated crackers can sound.

I knew who it was. I just didn't know what to say. "Dad?" I asked again.

I could tell he was calling from somewhere far away with horns honking in the background and conversations drifting past. I had a hard time hearing him. He got a few words out; then a garbage truck started backing up, beeping. "Dammit," he said, as he turned away from the phone. The noise frustrated him, and his frustration distracted him.

"Dad?" I said for the third time. It was like using a foreign word.

I always knew my father would resurface. He wasn't like the very bad fathers I had read about. You could always count on the newspaper to offer the worst compendium of parents, worse than yours, and I had searched for those stories as a means of comparison. Like the one who was arrested for child abuse after he left his kids in the car and went to the dog track and ate chateaubriand.

My father asked if I was watching out over Dwight. He was half asking and half reminding. "We don't call him that anymore," I said. "Now we call him Jim."

Then I hollered to my brother as loud as I could. Jim ran in, panting and sweaty.

"Is that Dad?" he said, trying to grab the phone. "Who is it?"

I gave him the phone and walked away.

His letters started to arrive. Coming home from school, I saw his big blocky handwriting on envelopes sticking out of my grandmother's mailbox. He must have been living in a halfway house in New Orleans but he never came out and said it. He alluded to his mysterious disappearance from our lives but never addressed it. He wrote to me as if I were still in the third grade; I was in the fifth grade and I craved candor and the truth.

The letters tried to drag me back in time, and that was not somewhere I wanted to go.

> *Anne, since I talked to you on the telephone that day, I have not heard from you or Dwight . . . I have been sick and this period has been one of the roughest in my life but they say I'm making progress in general and will be well soon.*

He didn't say who "they" was. "They" sounded serious. "They" sounded like a team of people working night and day to save my father. He didn't sound too good.

AFTER MORE phone calls, it got worked out that my mother would bring my brother and me to Hopewell and Plant City to visit Dad's family. We went on a sweltering Saturday. It was a reverse journey back to where we once were. They would all be there—Gigi, Big Nanny, all the elders, Uncle Roy and Aunt Dot and the cousins. We'd had no contact with them since we left. I could see my mother's resolve as we drove across the long bridge over Tampa Bay.

As we reached Hopewell, an old scene came back into focus. The black mailbox, our tires crunching over the coquina shell driveway as we rode beneath the promenade of towering oaks. Right at the gate, there was the old lawn jockey with a lantern there to guide you up the driveway.

When I was younger, I called him Jack, and I would sit in the grass and stare at him and try to understand the indefinable power he had.

I imagined the relatives didn't want us. I felt nervous, like we were charity cases. But the fragrance of the groves steadied me. After an uneasy dinner, we drove to Big Nanny's house in town for a perfunctory visit.

Big Nanny's bloodhound eyes drooped down even farther than before. She'd gotten slower, shuffling across the powder blue carpet as she made her way to the kitchen. Phoebe was at the stove stirring a pot of grits in her white uniform. Phoebe came to Big Nanny's a few times a week. Phoebe first worked for my great-aunt Donna, who was Big Nanny's daughter. When Aunt Donna became pregnant with her first child, she figured she'd need some help in the house. She got in her Buick and drove to Plant City's Black neighborhood, where Phoebe happened to be sitting on her porch. Phoebe was just as pregnant as Aunt Donna, who hired her on the spot. She started with Aunt Donna right away and stayed for sixty years. She had high cheekbones and a monk's ability to tune out the constant nattering when anyone else would have stuck their head in the oven.

If Big Nanny drove Phoebe crazy, she didn't show it. "My, my," she said as she watched Big Nanny rifle through her kitchen drawers for a spoon she couldn't find. I downright resented Big Nanny by then; she had deserted us in the wake of my father's collapse. I could still hear the sound of all those perforated checks she tore off her checkbook ledger to give my father, but there wasn't a single one ripped out for us.

Papa was dead, but his vibrating chair was still in the living room. I vibrated in it for a few minutes while the adults talked, then sidled out to the garage. The croquet mallets we used to play with were lined up in their wire rack. I chose one and took it out to the yard.

Big Nanny's lawn jockey was next to the birdbath and flowering hibiscus. He'd been trapped there as a lawn ornament his entire life, ageless and grinning, with absolutely no say in the matter. He could never get mad. He could never leave his tuft of grass. He grinned at me as I walked toward him with the croquet mallet. I'd never played golf, but I'd swung at enough baseballs. I teed up and swung, freeing the jockey from spending one more second outside the house with powder blue carpet inside. His shattered head went flying in pieces into the bushes. I didn't stick around long enough to look. I had to get that mallet back in the croquet set and pretend I'd never touched it.

CHAPTER 19

When Damie invited me to take the bus with her one afternoon, I was ready before she'd even finished talcing her boobs with lily of the valley. She said Mr. Falana would be picking us up shortly. We walked to the bus stop and sat on the bench beneath her parasol until the hydraulic brakes hissed in front of us and the doors opened.

"Well hell-oo, Mr. Falana!" My grandmother closed her parasol and climbed into the bus. I was the youngest passenger by forty years. Mr. Falana had to get up from the driver's seat to help other passengers off the bus. He seemed to know who had wobbles and who had darkness closing in around the edges of their vision. No one asked for his help; he had a sense when to move in. In an instant he was beside them, with his hand on an elbow or a shoulder and saying in a calm and deep voice, "Take your time." Everything was fine until they stood at the top of the stairs and suddenly three stairs seemed like the Grand Canyon. We stopped every three or four blocks. "The man is a saint, dealing with geriatrics all day," my grandmother said.

Mr. Falana dropped us off in an abandoned area of empty boutiques and shoe stores. The owners must have gone out for lunch in 1942 and never come back, only no one told the mannequins. They were still in the windows, missing arms or lying facedown in yellow newspaper. One storefront had dozens of Styrofoam heads in the window under a sign that read WIG VILLA. When I asked my grandmother why we'd gotten off the bus in such a creepy place, she smiled. "Dahling, we're in downtown St. Pete!"

We walked a few blocks toward a huge building with a red neon sign burning brighter than the hot yellow sun: WEBB'S CITY—WORLD'S MOST UNUSUAL DRUG STORE. Below it was a half-naked mermaid on a pink clamshell with a sign promising a FREE MERMAID SHOW.

The front entrance of Webb's was a massive bottleneck of shopping carts and wheelchairs. We fell in with the elderly crowd, and a jet-force fan sucked us inside into a retail fantasia of Bermuda shorts, surgical supplies, hearing aids, lipstick, hot nuts, straw handbags, caftans, ashtrays that fit inside a woman's purse, and parakeets, two for five dollars. There was a dry cleaner inside, a dance studio, a butcher, a seafood department, a florist, a coffee-roasting plant, and a small bank. We dodged the crowds to get to the lunch counter that went on forever.

A waitress came over as we sat down. "How ya doin' today, Ollie?" she asked my grandmother. "The usual?" A few minutes later she was back with a chocolate malt and cheese crackers.

After lunch, my grandmother went to look at girdles and directed me to the live mermaids on the fourth floor.

I crossed the gangplank and stepped up to the fake lava cave. I stuck my face into a porthole cut out of the papier-mâché grotto. There were the mermaids—a bunch of mannequins with fish tails instead of legs sitting around on some Reynolds Wrap. They were naked from the waist up with long hair covering their plastic breasts. A flirtatious female voice came over the speaker. "How old are you?" I looked around: "Me?" A fake mermaid with an otherworldly voice was speaking to me. "Do you swim in the ocean?"

I started taking the No. 16 bus to Webb's by myself to see the mermaids. I figured out the voice came from a woman sitting in a hidden box off to the side. I couldn't see her, but she could see me. The mermaids and their faraway stares were unreachable and yet they looked so content. They were just lounging around a treasure chest, a little tribe of them together at the bottom of the sea. I liked seeing them though I couldn't articulate why. This was still a safe period of naivete, before the teletype machine inside me started pounding out the reason.

MY GRANDMOTHER and I loved Carly Simon. Damie said that Carly was a nice Jewish girl from the Bronx who went to Sarah Lawrence. At night we waited for WLCY to play "You're So Vain." The guitar chords at the beginning of the song hinted of danger and secrecy, it was spine-tingling, and yet every time, the deejay trampled right over it with his talk, reminding us that Mick Jagger was on backup vocals or that Carly was married to James Taylor. "Shut up," I'd say from my bed. My grandmother brought home the latest *Rolling Stone* for me with an album review for *No Secrets*. I stared at the cover of the album. Carly was so cool—tawny and confident, wearing a maroon suede hat that matched her jeans, a thin blue shirt, and no bra.

I needed to see it in person. I took the No. 22 bus by myself to the mall and found Camelot Music across from Aladdin's Castle arcade. I shuffled through the *S*s, very casually, until Carly on the *No Secrets* cover stared me in the face. Just then, a greaseball clerk came up behind me and asked if I needed help. Heart racing, I flipped forward to Paul Simon and said no thanks. It took a second trip to Camelot to get up the courage to buy the album. The greaseball wasn't working. When the cashier put *No Secrets* in a bag, I asked her to double bag it.

SEX WAS suddenly everywhere. A young couple moved in across the street from my grandmother's house. They lowered the median age by thirty years. They needed a babysitter, and being the only other female in the neighborhood under seventy, I got the job. My first night there, I put the two kids down for bed and was sitting in the living room when I spotted *The Joy of Sex* in their magazine basket. It wasn't hidden or disguised or anything; it was just sticking out of the wicker basket next to *Newsweek*. I wondered if it was a trap. I wiped my fingertips on the shag carpet so I wouldn't leave smudge marks on the pages and I moved away from the living room window.

All that precaution and *The Joy of Sex* was nothing but feathery sketches of a naked man and woman demonstrating different contortions. They both had long hair. Tangled up as they were, it was hard to tell who was who and doing what to whom. There wasn't a single photo in the book. I'd seen worse in the *National Geographic*.

Outside, the wind kicked up, and the wind chimes on the porch went hysterical. Shrubs scratched the side of the house. A small pebble hit the window. It was past eleven and *Alfred Hitchcock Presents* came on, a terrifying episode about a man who wakes up to find a venomous snake curled up on his stomach. I sat frozen in the corduroy recliner, too scared to get up and turn off the TV. The minutes dragged by. I vowed to never babysit again. I hated babysitting. I'd go back to mowing yards or scamming the elderly. If it weren't for the two children asleep in their bedroom, I would have run home. I heard a key in the door and the voices of the young couple—I was safe. Then I saw *The Joy of Sex* wasn't put back.

A FEW weeks later, I was walking home from school, wearing my St. Paul's low-slung skirt, carrying my notebook on my hip, when a car idled alongside of me. It squeaked like busted bed springs. Maybe a Cadillac or a Lincoln. At the stop sign, I waited for the car to move on so I could cross the street. It didn't move. The windows were open. I looked down into the car and saw the driver's hand doing something.

It was hard to see what because his fat stomach hung over his belt. What a birdbrain, the man left his house not wearing any pants! But he had tan pants on; they were just pulled down. His hand was also tan, moving faster. He looked right at me, bored into my eyes, as if he'd waited his whole life to see fear in a child's face, and then, his muffler getting louder, he drove away.

I stared at his license plate and repeated the number out loud again and again as I looked around for a stick to write it down in the dirt like they said. I was still holding my spiral notebook. I couldn't find a stick, so I started running as fast as I could to my grandmother's house. I cut through yards so he wouldn't find me, zigzagging under clotheslines. A raggedy muffler sounded in the distance and I kept running, losing a little more of the license plate number with each step. Some old person screamed at me to stay off their grass.

Even our front yard felt dangerous. The police rolled up in front of our house to take a report after my grandmother called them. Damie offered the cops some ginger ale. We sat in the living room, me in my St. Paul's uniform. I was mad at myself for forgetting the license number and not being able to give a good description and for not getting away from the man sooner. That man was a sicko, everybody said it.

What exactly was a sicko?

NOT LONG after that, an eighty-year-old neighbor was raped in her home. Police detectives were in and out of the house all day. My grandmother and I watched the activity from our glider swing. We had the afternoon paper on our laps. It had just been delivered and we'd split it up for reading, but neither of us was reading. The cops were starting to clear out. The lady was a grouch who edged her yard every week and had three big rose bushes in a little stone area near her door. She wouldn't have appreciated the pieces of yellow crime scene tape the police left on the porch. Good that she didn't see it. I asked my grandmother again for more details. She explained the nature of unwanted sex, which wasn't sex at all, she said, but violence. I didn't understand how something as small as a penis could be used as a weapon.

Damie offered her final remarks in her aristocratic accent: "A stiff prick knows no conscience."

CHAPTER 20

Uncle Rod fell in love with a woman who worked at a vitamin store. She was a health buff with a petite build and blond windswept hair. I'd see her and think, Hey, it's Angie Dickinson from *Police Woman* smoking a lettuce cigarette with my uncle Rod. He sprinkled wheat germ on everything and started to look for his own place. It took him about ten minutes to find one, a 1920s efficiency apartment with birds-of-paradise on the outside and a courtyard full of down-and-outers on the inside.

We didn't know he was leaving until his two friends from AA showed up to help. There was hardly anything to move—some clothes and books, his shaving gear, an electric fan, a beach chair, a car wax kit, and the commercial coffee urn he'd lifted from Moock's. His AA buddies were house painters. They had paint-speckled arms and weathered faces, as if someone forgot to bring them inside. My grandmother said they were there to support Uncle Rod and wasn't it a beautiful thing. Uncle Rod sure seemed okay to me. He practically laid rubber backing out of our driveway.

*   *   *

I REMEMBER the exact moment I realized that we might leave too. It was the sound of a shopping bag rattling in my mother's bedroom. A high-quality department store bag. I ran in there and saw two new blouses. One had short sleeves and was black with little hippie flower bouquets on it, very snappy. My mother had recently been promoted to assistant principal of an elementary school. Our money wasn't as tight. My brother even went away to an overnight summer camp for a week. It was near a prison, with leaky canoes and powdered eggs, but camp was camp, and he was a boy in the woods whose letters home went on for two pages describing the wilderness and camaraderie.

The rattling of the new shopping bag meant we were getting back on our feet. The sound filled me with dread.

I began to notice small things. My mother never referred to my grandmother's house as "home." She called it "Mama's house." We were driving along one afternoon and she said such and such about "Mama's house." I whipped around in the torn bucket seat of the Cutlass. "You mean, home?"

I could have asked her if she was happy at my grandmother's house, but I was too afraid of the answer. No way could I go back to the nine-year-old who arrived at Damie's house, when I wet my pajamas and ducked for cover anytime a car engine backfired. I needed the healing environment of Tibetan singing bowls, Guatemalan handicrafts, and oyster crackers in the cushions where my grandmother sat as she held down our fort.

I could ask my grandmother anything. She was in the glider swing one afternoon when I came home from my guitar lesson at Mr. Nicolosi's house across the street. He was in a jazz trio and led a big band orchestra that played all over town. When I showed him the sheet music to "Smoke on the Water," he balled it up and said it was for morons.

Her face was vaguely serene as we swayed gently back and forth under the banyan tree. Since she was the old one, I used my foot to keep us going. I asked her if she liked us living with her, a softball question, but the answer was good to hear anyway: "Of course, dahling."

I asked if she thought my mother liked living at her house, and her face maintained the same zen. "Your mother has a ball everywhere she goes," she said, dismissing the silly question with a wave of the hand.

The possibility that my mother wasn't sold on the life we'd built at my grandmother's made me wonder how it could be better.

We had everything we could have wanted. We had a bread-winner, and Damie counted as a half parent. We had good friends, St. Paul's was three blocks away, and my mother had finally gotten what she'd wanted ever since our days of getting stuck in the sand at the fleabag apartment in Sebring: a AAA auto club membership with courtesy towing in a twenty-five-mile radius.

And yet it seemed like the more security we gained, the more restless my mother became. We had a once-a-month tradition of going to Morrison's Cafeteria for dinner. At Morrison's, they let you pick your own food. You slid your plastic tray down a long silver railing and right in front of you was Salisbury steak, baked chicken, ham, corn, whipped potatoes with gravy; whatever you wanted, you just reached for, even

the cakes and pies at the end. The first night we could afford
to go to Morrison's, my mother took a bite of Salisbury steak
and said, "Chew slowly and savor." Once, when she and my
grandmother and I sat down at our table—my brother had
a Scout meeting—Mom beamed at us and raised a glass of
water. "Three generations of women, out to dinner, have we
made it, or what?" But Morrison's didn't excite her as much
anymore. She had a Fresca and a side salad and smoked while
I ate butterscotch pudding in a parfait glass.

Maybe it was me. I committed to being a better daughter.
I folded the towels like she asked. I stopped cutting articles
out of the newspaper before she read them. When someone
phoned for her, I wrote down their information instead of
pretending I was Chinese.

ONE AFTERNOON a giant red Coca-Cola truck was
parked in front of my grandmother's house when I came
home from school. All kinds of people stopped by to visit
Damie during the day, but we'd never had a fifty-foot Coke
truck. A man with dark hair came out of the house. He wore
a red-and-white-striped shirt with his name stitched in red
cursive letters over the pocket: "Donny."

"Hi there, you must be Vicki's daughter," he said, his
green eyes shimmering in the sunlight. "I'm Donny."

"It says it on your shirt," I said, holding my schoolbooks
tighter. He smiled. "Right," he said. He climbed back into his
rig and waved goodbye, ten thousand glass bottles of Coke
trembling behind him. I raced into the house and asked my
grandmother who Donny was.

She said he was the brother of one of Mom's high school

friends. He'd stopped by hoping to catch my mother—but he'd try her on the phone after work one night.

My mother got lots of calls at night. Parents called to discuss an issue with their child, especially the single parents who worked one or two jobs. This is how I learned of her near-encyclopedic knowledge of other people's children. When she said their names, it was as if she'd known them all their lives: "Ray will pull through this, the same way he did after his grandfather died." She took the calls from a wobbly card table in her bedroom, where it was hot and airless from the waxy palm fronds that choked off her window. On the table, she had her notes on each child and a pack of Marlboros. If the parents were talkers, she discreetly lit a cigarette and side-piped the smoke from the corner of her mouth.

One single mother who didn't have a phone at home called from her job at the bowling alley. My mom had to shout over the noise of twenty lanes of bowling balls crashing into pins.

I never thought of my mother as a single mother. Single moms had hard lives and worked at bowling alleys and limped along without a man in the house. We had my grandmother and two newspapers delivered a day and *The Carol Burnett Show* on Saturday night, when my mother broke her zipper laughing and I fixed everyone bowls of orange sherbet during the commercials.

Donny called a few nights later. On this call she stretched the cord as far as it would go into her room and closed the door. My room was on the other side of the wall. I put my ear to the plaster, trying to listen from my bed. I couldn't make out the words she said, but the tone of her voice sounded like the mermaids at Webb's City, underwater and ethereal. She was still on the phone when I fell asleep.

The next Saturday night, she went out on a date with Donny. She said she'd be home by eleven at the latest. My grandmother and I watched *The Carol Burnett Show* without her. Everything was wrong. Usually, I sat in the butterfly chair, but I moved up to the empty spot on the couch, stretching my legs out until my toes touched Damie. Unsolicited, she gave me a foot massage trying to distract me from watching the clock on the wall by the front door.

MY MOTHER decided to attend a Parents Without Partners picnic. As a sixth grader, I wanted no part of it. We weren't picnic types. My mother didn't even like the outdoors. The real sting was that the life we lived was insufficient for my mother, so much so that she would attend a picnic for a lonely hearts group with a lonely name.

"It will be an experience," she said in a breezy voice. "It will be an experience" is what she said when she wanted me to try a bite of a hundred-year egg at China City. I didn't want an experience. I wanted fried rice. I wanted to keep our routine of watching *Soul Train* while my mother colored her hair in the pink sink in my grandmother's bathroom. Instead, she put on her new blouse and dragged Jim and me to the picnic.

We got to Lake Seminole, a typical public park with balloons strung around the picnic shelters. Untypical was the huge sign on one shelter: WELCOME PARENTS WITHOUT PARTNERS.

Oh my God, they were practically advertising it! I had assumed it would be like the Al-Anon meeting my mother took us to where the location was hush-hush and unmarked, and we had to go around a building pulling on doors until the right one opened. Parents Without Partners didn't care who they tainted by association. They hung up a banner screaming out that we were at a dented-can convention.

We walked toward the sea of divorcées who had brought their kids—all so the adults could see what they might be getting with the package. I had a bad feeling about this organization. Unlike Donny from Coca-Cola, the picnic people were seriously spouse-shopping.

CHAPTER 21

When *The Exorcist* came out, my grandmother and I watched the evening news showing grainy clips of spinning heads and smoking bile oozing from the mouth of the possessed girl, as Catholics protested outside movie theaters across the country. Meanwhile, my mother accepted a date with a man from the picnic, a divorced accountant raising two kids.

Ted took my mother to dinner at St. Pete's only French restaurant. He ordered escargots and quizzed the waiter on wines from the Burgundy region. He wasn't bad looking. He shared his interests in rare coins and rare stamps.

It would take a few more months for Ted to reveal himself to be the cheapskate who looked for coins at the beach with a metal detector. As a weekend treat, he bought us kids expired Entenmann's Danish from the day-old bread store. My mother noted his quirks, but she liked having someone who cared for her. After ten months of dating, he proposed marriage. He was eager to combine families—her two kids and his two kids—for a total of four kids under the age of thirteen.

*   *   *

MY MOTHER was confronted with two choices: marry a man she didn't love or accept a possible future of being unloved and alone. She ran through the pros and cons every afternoon in the parking lot of McDonald's. She sat in her car and wrote in her spiral journal that she wasn't in love with Ted but blamed herself. Why couldn't she love someone? Maybe real love wasn't possible, at least not the kind she'd always dreamed of. In her journals, she reminded herself of Ted's positive qualities: intelligent, income earner, and seemingly stable.

On my thirteenth birthday, I gashed my foot on a big conch shell at the beach. Ted's miserly solution was to pour a bottle of iodine on the gushing wound. My mother and I ended up in the emergency room at St. Anthony's Hospital for five stitches and lingering pain from the iodine burn. In the ER, we had to wait two hours for the nurse to call us back. The whole time, my mother kept her hand on my leg and glanced at the bloody towel around my foot. It was a great birthday.

Mom wrote in her spiral notebook remembering that thirteen years ago on this night she was in a different hospital with a different man, with the birth of their first child suggesting a life full of promise. Nothing turned out as expected: now she was a divorced mother of two with ambivalent feelings for a new man who was promising her a new life. It was now or never, before Ted met someone who thought he was the world's greatest catch.

After six weeks of soul-searching, she caved. She and Ted told me the news together. Ted did the talking while my mother looked at the floor. I sobbed. I pleaded. I kicked over a wastebasket and alluded to unforeseen circumstances that might disrupt the wedding. Ted leapt up from his chair and said, "Are you threatening me?" I looked past him, at my mother, who was on the verge of tears herself.

I begged her to let me stay at my grandmother's house and go to eighth grade at St. Paul's. Instead, the wedding was held at St. Paul's. My mother wore a cream-colored muslin dress and Ted gave her a jade-and-gold wedding ring.

The next day we moved to Ted's house fifteen long miles away in the armpit of the county in a soggy subdivision of cul-de-sacs and dented garage doors. There weren't any city buses. I was cut off from the world, in a house with swords on the walls. Ted had a huge bank safe in his dining room. It was five feet tall and three feet wide, with a combination lock like you saw in bank heist movies where they blow the door off with a stick of dynamite. It was covered by a plastic floral tablecloth.

He tried to establish himself as boss of the house, drawing up a matrix of chores for each of us on graph paper. It made no sense to scrub a bathroom every day, and when I shared that with him, he actually said, "If I wanted your opinion, I would ask for it."

When I asked him why he bothered having children in the first place, he took it as smart-mouth. Ted didn't appreciate kids who talked back; I didn't appreciate bullies, so I spent the first six months on restriction in my bedroom. As I told Ted, I welcomed the escape. My brother snuck in batteries for my transistor radio so I could listen to the Carpenters and feel the full weight of my suffering. If it weren't for Karen Carpenter, I never would have survived those months.

Once, as punishment, I had to mow the backyard, a quarter acre of shin-high grass that sloped down to a ditch, with

Ted's old push mower. He came back hours later to inspect my work. He stood on the second-story balcony to get a better view, and from there he read the message I mowed for him.

FUCK U

He got even madder when he took my mother to the balcony to show her and she laughed. She quickly put her hand over her mouth to contain the damage. Ted said no wonder I was a spoiled brat and it would never work if my mother continued to undercut his parenting. I spent another two weeks in my bedroom with the Carpenters.

MY MOTHER tried to placate us both. She made beef bourguignon for Ted and went to the flea market with him on the weekends. He loved strolling the dirt aisles perusing ten-packs of men's socks for three dollars. My mother took me on secret outings after she came home from school. We'd go to a shopping center for a milkshake or look at magazines at the drugstore. "This is our time," she'd say, both of us understanding that if Ted found out he'd berate her for spoiling me.

ON WEEKENDS Ted made us go with him to the Wagon Wheel Flea Market. It was a hundred acres of heat and dust, everyone packed in tight and eyeing others with mistrust—all for a used hand mixer encrusted with someone else's egg whites. My stomach got sick just looking at the wares.

"You're welcome to stay in the car," Ted said. I stayed in the car and killed time by writing little character sketches of his Wagon Wheel brethren I saw out the window.

If my mother could swing it, she'd drop me off at Damie's house for the weekend. I'd have my own bed back and she'd make us her special milkshakes with an egg, nutmeg, and cinnamon. I'd hop the bus to Webb's City with friends from St. Paul's, joining in as they used straws to shoot spitballs at the mermaid exhibit sign, disavowing my past—and myself.

Most Saturdays, though, my brother and I watched wrestling on TV broadcast live from Tampa. I was thirteen and too old to be watching Terry Funk put Andre the Giant in headscissors, but my life was over anyway, so why not stay shut inside on a sunny Saturday.

Jim was just beginning to accept the possibility that the wrestling was staged. We sat on the living room rug, up close to the TV, and I spent the hour snuffing out his last hope that the wrestling was real. "Then why is it called 'professional' wrestling?" he said. Besides, the matches were broadcast live. "They wouldn't have time to make it fake!"

After wrestling, we watched *Creature Feature* with Dr. Paul Bearer. Wearing theatrical makeup, a fake scar, gargoyle eyes, and formal black tails, he hosted the Saturday afternoon horror movie on local TV. I was wasting away.

One Saturday afternoon, I was changing channels and tennis came on. Not normal tennis, but a holy kind of tennis, with an emerald-green grass court and hushed silence as two women in white skirts whacked the hell out of the ball. It was Wimbledon. It was the era of Chris Evert and Björn Borg and Billie Jean King, with her shag haircut and aviator glasses. That's it! I decided on the spot: I would devote my life to tennis and become a professional tennis player. I found an old racket in Ted's garage and started hitting balls against the side of the house.

AS I got older, my fights with Ted created tension between him and my mother, but I kept testing my mother, hoping she'd choose me, and never getting a clear answer.

Ted's interest in rare stamps and coins meant he would spend hours in his rat-pack den, drinking tawny port and blasting Mahler on a school night. He liked bombastic requiems that built to a frenzy—German chanting and ominous timpani drums, anything that sounded like someone was being boiled alive at Carnegie Hall.

His den was next to my bedroom. I yelled for him to please turn it down. Nothing. I pounded on my bedroom wall. He ignored me. I stormed out to the hallway and screamed across the house to my mother: "Mom, it's a SCHOOL NIGHT." She went into the den. I couldn't hear what they were saying over the crashing cymbals. A few minutes later, Ted relented and turned down the volume.

"What an asshole," I said to my mother as she left the den.

As a family, we were hanging by a thread. The thread was Sunday dinner. It was the one night in the week that my working mother cooked. She started cooking early on Sunday afternoon—salteado or a standing rib roast—chopping onions and splashing Spanish sherry in pans as Julio Iglesias belted out songs of passion from the cassette deck on the kitchen counter.

She brought out her Mexican serving dishes and silver butter knives from antique stores and etched wine glasses in different shapes and sizes. While she cooked, Ted went to get my grandmother and bring her back for dinner. At 6 p.m. Ted and I entered a brief truce—four teenagers, Damie, Ted, and my mom sat down at the table. My mother explained each dish as we passed the serving platters around. Wait, she said, let me get the camera. Ted told her to sit down and enjoy the meal, but she came back with her camera, and then she had to adjust the light. By then we'd all be yelling at her to sit down so we could eat. Finally, she took the picture. Then she would survey us and the beautiful table. "Bon appétit, family," she'd say.

The rest of the week, we dispersed in the wind. I ate dinner at Ponderosa Steakhouse, where I worked part-time; my brother ate soft-serve ice cream at Carvel, where he worked. Since my mother didn't want me riding my ten-speed home from Ponderosa at 10:30 p.m. in a red-checked cowgirl uniform, she or Ted had to come get me. I hated owing him anything. I tried to pay him for the ride. Each time he'd decline, sighing wearily, as if I didn't know anything about the world.

THE SUMMER before tenth grade, my tennis coach landed a job as the teaching pro at a swanky tennis club in Myrtle Beach. He offered me free room and board in exchange for helping run a kids' tennis camp. He was twenty-five but seemed older, probably because he was used to yelling at adults to get their rackets back.

My mother signed off on the trip. She saw it for what it was—my chance to escape. She bought me a suitcase on sale, and when she presented it to me, she asked if she could go too.

I had just turned sixteen, and for the next two weeks, I slept on a foam mattress on the floor next to my sneakers and suitcase. The younger brother of my coach, who was also a tennis pro, was camped out in another room. We overlooked a dozen pristine clay tennis courts. We didn't have much furniture—a couch, beds, a table, and chairs—mostly the place had sweatbands and headbands on doorknobs and counters and scattered across the carpet. Eighty percent of the condo was terry cloth.

It was ecstasy. We listened to "Barracuda" at full volume while we ate breakfast. At night, my coach drank a foreign beer out of a green bottle called Heineken while we listened to Bowie's *Diamond Dogs*. The brothers wore Fila tennis shirts, like Björn Borg, and occasionally walked through the condo shirtless, their white chests shaped like a tennis shirt where the sun never hit. The rest was coppery brown skin and golden hair on muscled limbs. I'd never seen men up close before.

On the last day in Myrtle Beach, I took one of their sweatbands from the laundry basket and put it in my suitcase. Back home in St. Pete, I filled my journal with daydreams about the brothers and our life in the condo and the life I wanted some day. I wanted to listen to "Barracuda" at breakfast and wear Fila shirts and drink beer in a green bottle with a label in a foreign language.

THAT SPRING I played a tennis tournament an hour and a half from St. Pete. The mother of another teammate drove four of us. She crossed the bridge to Tampa and then left the interstate for a back road to Lakeland.

We saw a big black hearse on the side of the road. It was old-timey looking, like on *The Munsters*. A huge man wearing a black tux and a white dress shirt was changing the tire with a jack. It was Dr. Paul Bearer, the hammy host of *Creature Feature*. We were hysterical. We were still looking back at him, laughing, when I realized where we were. We were coming up on Aunt Dot's fruit stand. There it was under the oak tree. It was closed for summer. I saw the Hull groves all around it and somewhere in there were my father's thirteen acres of trees. I was back in the ancient moss spooled in the ancient oaks at Hopewell and oranges dropping through the windows of my father's Ford. I felt very quiet for a few seconds and was glad when the fruit stand and Hopewell were behind us.

DAD CONTINUED to call and write to me from afar.

After my mom packed up the car the day we left for St. Pete, my father stayed drunk for two years, destitute, living in cheap hotels and dry-out places before getting sober. The letters came from all over—the port of New Orleans, where he was a security guard, the Rio Grande Valley, where he'd gone to work the Texas citrus season. He wrote about mountain lions and how different they were from anything we had in Florida. It was hard not to get drawn into his colorful accounts, but every letter eventually got around to how sorry he was for disappearing from our lives and he wanted more than anything to make it up. I wasn't interested in the past.

> *It was so good to talk with you yesterday for more reasons than you know. It's like beginning to feel very clean inside . . . [Damie] says that you are old enough to*

understand things and to write to you and tell you the way things are with me and how I feel about you. This is to do that and let you know that I am with you in spirit on your birthday. I've started so many letters to you and Dwight and never mailed them because I have been ashamed to tell you I had no money to send you or was not in a good job. It was not because I did not want to write or send money to you.

You are my daughter and your pictures and letters are beautiful. I am very proud of all your accomplishments. You reflect yourself and your mother's care. You would make any father proud.

I don't remember saving the letter or any of the others he sent to me. And yet one day I'd pry open a musty black trunk and find the entire stack in their original envelopes, preserved by a mystery archivist that had to be me.

CHAPTER 22

Over the years I saw my father only sporadically, in awkward meetings that he initiated, in coffee shops that were too loud for him or in traffic that moved too fast for his junker car. My mother and Damie said the visits meant more to him than I probably knew. I didn't look forward to them. Our conversations consisted of pauses, silences, and both of us starting a sentence at the same time.

"Pardon me, go ahead."

"No, my fault, you go ahead."

"I didn't mean to interrupt you."

"I think you were first. What did you want to say?"

"I was going to respond to something you said."

"Oh. What was it?"

Somehow, some way, he came up with the funds to pay for my first year of college at FSU, his alma mater. I wouldn't have accepted five hundred bucks from my stepfather if he'd offered, but I'd take four thousand dollars off a man whose eyeglasses were held together with a bent staple. I didn't let myself feel too bad about it. He was my father. He told me he could only cover the first year. That worked out fine. I only made it that far.

In late summer, my mother drove me up to FSU in Tallahassee. It was five hours of cow pastures, speed traps, and prison towns. It was the longest we'd spent alone since she married Ted. She helped me set up my dorm room, and we said a teary goodbye.

Two of my friends from high school had signed up to go through sorority rush at FSU, so I did too. The August heat and humidity were brutal, and the gently rolling hills of the FSU campus were not so gentle in the cheap strappy sandals I was not used to wearing. The white-columned antebellum mansions all looked the same. I trudged from sorority house to sorority house, my feet raw with blisters and my mascara melted into a harlequin clown pattern on my face. I never knew where I was. I mixed up the Greek letters and mistakenly praised the wrong sorority during light banter. At the Tri Delt house, a sorority of Southern blond beauties, I thought a girl would call for my execution when I confused her sorority with a sorority known for Saturday movie nights with hot fudge sundaes. Her bronze face went dead. She glanced at the sweat stains under my arms and spun away.

Rush week made Jackie's School of Dance seem like a party compared to the killing fields of beautiful creatures with laser eyes and add-a-bead necklaces. I was desperate to be a part of those killing fields.

I was rejected by all three of my top choices. "Try again next year!" said one xeroxed form letter. I'd worked two jobs that summer to pay for new sundresses and sandals.

I called my mother sobbing from a pay phone on campus.

"Oh, my darling girl," she said. I could hear the ache in her voice. She'd known rejection. After I blubbered for a while and we were about to hang up, she offered Damie's wise words for whenever the shit hit the fan. "This, too, shall pass," she told me.

BACK HOME over the Christmas break, I took a burger-flipping job for extra money. My grill partner was an unusual woman with cerulean-blue eyes who spoke in puns and riddles. At the end of my first day, Blue Eyes asked if I'd be back in the morning, as if I'd just stopped by to make grilled cheese sandwiches for eight hours.

"Uh, yeah," I said.

We turned out to be a good team. When the orders were stacked up, we rushed past and around each other in familiar glide patterns, never once colliding. The first week flew by. In a lull one afternoon, she was telling me a story about a blue whale she'd seen while crewing a sailboat off the coast of Maine. Just then, a customer, a Porsche-driving doctor in town, interrupted us to try and impress her with a story about his sailboat. She turned to him and smiled, briefly, then returned her full attention to our whale story.

Blue Eyes was in her early thirties. She was scant on personal details, even elusive, and what few details she shared came out as incidental asides. When the Coke and Sprite taps on the soda machine at work broke, she mentioned a drink cart that nearly turned over on a plane to Mexico City when she was a flight attendant with Braniff Airways. There was no time to dig in further; we were on to the next topic, laughing and ignoring customers. It was like rolling down a hill together.

I started having dizzy spells. I forgot the fries in the fryer and set off the smoke alarm. My boss, a gem of a lady and a steel magnolia, took me aside. "Honey, what's wrong with you?" she asked.

My days off dragged. The hours inched along, as I hung out with friends, drinking their parents' Christmas party booze, waiting until it was time to put on my hairnet for work.

We were down to our last few shifts before Christmas break ended. I was at the counter, taking a customer's order when Blue Eyes came up behind me and touched the back of my leg, a playful mischievous hello, right behind the knee. My leg bones turned to feathers. I grabbed onto the counter.

Blue Eyes suggested we go to one of her favorite places, called the Wedgwood Inn. I'd never heard of it. We arrived at an old motel with Mexican jasmine crawling around it and an empty parking lot. It looked as if it had been closed for decades, but it had a whiff of grandeur, separate from the rest of the world. For Blue Eyes, the Wedgwood had the added perk that no one but old ladies went there, so there would be little chance of her running into anyone she knew.

I had a sense of déjà vu, as if falling into a familiar and mysterious trance. We were a half mile from Webb's City, where I had gone to stare at the mermaids with their tinfoil tails when I was thirteen. At the Wedgwood, I had something better than a mermaid, sitting on the other side of the booth from me, sipping a Chablis.

The night before I went back to school, Blue Eyes asked me out to dinner. Afterward we sat in the dark in her car. She moved closer to me. I moved closer to her. We got closer and closer until we kissed, and kept kissing. We made out for an hour. All of the puzzle pieces that had been missing were found. The pieces fit together.

She drove me home, and we stayed in her car in my driveway, making out for another two hours. My mother came outside to let the dog out before going to bed. Or to check on me. Either way, she got what was going on.

I didn't sleep all night. When my ride came the next morning, I said goodbye to my mom by shouting, "Mom, maybe I'm gay. I don't know!"

I rode back to FSU, still smelling like Blue Eyes's perfume, Opium. It kept me company in a car full of friends on a five-hour drive back to a place I didn't want to go.

I blew through the next semester waiting by the mailbox for her letters. One arrived with a few grains of beach sand in the envelope. Maybe it was a message that she wanted to take me to the sandbar she liked. Maybe sand had a hidden meaning between two women. Maybe a beach was a place where no one would see her writing a letter to a lovesick eighteen-year-old. I spun out the myriad possibilities while I listened to Joni Mitchell in my dorm room. The big fat chapter on Descartes in my philosophy textbook went unread. Blue Eyes had strongly suggested I not call or write because she had a roommate.

I don't think she expected me to come home that next summer, but there I was, back at the grill. I should have spent the summer building houses for Habitat for Humanity or learning a foreign language in Guatemala. Instead, I flipped grilled cheese sandwiches and waited for a glass of Chablis. I was ready to flip grilled cheese sandwiches till the end of time if it meant being in her eau de toilette cloud of Opium.

And then she quit. She didn't have a roommate, as it

turned out. She had a live-in girlfriend. And the girlfriend was catching on that something was up.

I moped the whole summer. I waitressed during the day, carrying patty melts to the table with a dead soul. At night I borrowed my mother's car and drove around town in slow meandering loops past the places we used to go. All three of them. Then I drove by the places we'd talked about going, overwhelmed by the poignancy of what could have been. The tears came in the Arby's drive-through as I waited for my Jamocha shake.

In a rare crumb of disclosure, Blue Eyes once mentioned the name of an acoustic blues duo she'd gone to listen to one weekend. I checked the band listings in the paper until I found an ad for their next gig in town. The pub was dark and loud. I walked through the narrow corridors until I saw her in a cramped booth. She saw me and froze, her eyes turning into blue saucers. I waited until she got up to go to the bathroom and followed her in. I pushed her against the bathroom wall and we kissed in a tangled-up hurry. Then it was over; she left me at the paper towel dispenser. I watched her returning to the booth and to her girlfriend.

I needed my own wheels, a car that would restore my confidence. I got a second job at a financial investment firm, where all I had to do was stuff prospectuses into envelopes at night. Easy money, but after three nights of paper cuts, my hands had blown up to the size of baby lobsters. I went home and soaked them in salt water while looking at used sports cars in the local Auto Trader. The hands healed and my savings account grew.

Every Friday afternoon, it was me and five gearheads waiting outside the 7-Eleven for the latest Auto Trader to hit the racks. Soon, I was the proud owner of a cobalt blue MGB GT. The car had 152,000 miles and an oil leak, but it also had leather seats and a wood-grain steering wheel. I imagined pulling up to a red light and in the next lane would be Blue Eyes. What a coincidence. I'd wave fondly and drive off in a streak of cobalt.

I pulled up to a hundred traffic lights and never found her.

I DREADED returning to FSU for sophomore year. The place was jinxed, it was bad news, and I didn't belong. I couldn't even wear my FSU shower shoes in good conscience. Instead of going back, I enrolled at the junior college in St. Pete. I failed earth science twice and racked up nine hundred dollars in parking tickets.

I didn't know if I was gay. I didn't know any gay people, besides the drama teacher at my mother's school and the Village People. I didn't know where lesbians gathered or what kind of restaurants they liked. Searching for leads, I tuned into a local radio show called the *Women's Hour*. It was actually two hours. They discussed unsafe levels of aluminum in female deodorants, and then they played terrible music. The songs were about waterfalls and flowing rivers that finally spilled over. It made me anxious. All I wanted them to tell me was where I was supposed to go.

My tennis days were ancient history when I ran into a local tennis hotshot who came back into town. "Heyyyy," she said, as if she remembered fifteen-year-old me. She was long and lithe. She wore black Wayfarers and had the same thick shiny hair as a Kennedy on a sailboat. She suggested we grab a beer sometime. Her invitation was casual, but I turned it over in my mind for days. I wondered if there was a hidden meaning, and if so, what was it about me that triggered her suggestion? Was her sonar system pinging?

We met at El Cap, a St. Pete time-warped tavern where ballplayers came during spring training. I walked in, and it was all old geezers on bar stools until my friend arrived with her VW convertible–tousled hair and gold earrings. She was twenty-five and low-key cool; her entire personality saun-tered. Three hours and two pitchers of Miller Lite later, we were outside behind El Cap in a hedge of azaleas, the bark mulch stabbing me in the back. It was a long way from Cha-blis at the Wedgwood Inn.

JOB-WISE, FUTURE-WISE, there was no road map. I had no career vision, no college degree, and no calling. Being aimless and average at nineteen was excusable; at twenty-two, I was ready to grab any piece of driftwood floating by that might keep me from going under.

I took a job as a sales representative with Revlon in their beauty care division. My territory was all of Fort Lauderdale up to Boynton Beach calling on buyers at small retail chains to convince them they needed a thousand cases of Flex sham-poo. Revlon gave me a company car. It was a Ford Granada, a big square boat just like the car HP Hood gave my father to drive through the groves. Instead of oranges, my back seat was crowded with six-foot-tall beautiful women made of card-board. They were the Flex shampoo store displays. The women were so tall I had to fold them in half to close the car door.

I was back to driving around Florida in a goddamn Ford.

My relationship with my mother had frayed in the last year

or two. It was the same stuff we'd struggled over since she married Ted, with the additional X factor of my gayness. She was rattled after seeing me tangled up with Blue Eyes, but over time she'd gotten used to the idea. It was Ted who was a jerk. I brought a woman to their house one time. Granted, she was odd, a Slash look-alike with dark rocker hair who parked her taxi in our driveway. Ted banned her from future visits. "I don't want those kinds of people in my house," he told me. What kind of people? Lesbians in top hats? He probably meant a stranger who looked like she might steal his rare coin collection, but I took it as an assault on my sexuality, not to mention my taste in women.

I didn't expect my mother to march with PFLAG in a Pride parade, but I wanted her to share my outrage with Ted's comment. She didn't. I was old enough to say fuck that and stomped off.

While I was in Fort Lauderdale, my mother and I talked on the phone every week or two but more to confirm that both of us were still alive.

I HARDLY slept that year. I was terrified of everything in the dark. My apartment was in a seafoam green duplex in the side yard of an elderly woman's home, smothered by pygmy palms and a fuchsia jungle of flowering vines. The landlady was eighty-two and stalked through the yard with a machete in her hand scanning for bougainvillea to hack back.

I rented the place because it reminded me of my grandmother's house—the same jalousie windows and flimsy push-button door locks, even the same lizards that ran across window screens. I thought it would be like home. Here, it all felt menacing. My neighbors were burned-out drifters who walked to the store for beer. Random strangers knocked on my door asking to borrow my car. The county hospital was next to my apartment. At night, ambulances wailed in the distance, getting closer and louder until they were literally outside my bedroom window, which overlooked the ER.

It wasn't the sirens that woke me up though; it was the panic of knowing that in five hours I'd have to sell shampoo.

I DROVE to my sales calls in a short rayon skirt, a roll of Tums on the seat and a can of Diet Coke between my legs. I prayed for the buyers to cancel our appointment, but these people were never sick, their relatives never died, and their kids never had emergency dental surgery. They were always there, working their calculators faster than I could find the buttons on mine. "Come on, Revlon, stay with me!" one buyer said, not even looking up.

At the end of every two weeks, I was down to pennies because my boss was late filing my expense report. So was the Revlon rep in the territory south of me. Once we flew home from a sales meeting and didn't have enough money to get our car out of airport parking. We handed over a case of Flex shampoo. The parking attendant called it even and opened the gate.

To eat at night, we double-teamed all the happy hours with complimentary buffets. Mondays at Mai-Kai for teriyaki bites, Tuesdays at the Jolly Roger for Swedish meatballs, Wednesdays at Stan's for the stuffed mushrooms, and Thursdays at Cafe Martinique for stir-fry shrimp. We avoided happy hours that stipulated "Unescorted Ladies, please" because it was hard to eat in a shark tank.

On Fridays, I tagged along with Billy and Will, two gay guys who were kind enough to bring me with them to Backstreet during prime hunting hours. I was too chicken to go to the women's bar, so I continued to glom on to them until one of them, Billy or Will—I can't remember—said, "Time to fly, little bird."

The boys said go to Shangri-La, a lesbian bar in nearby Plantation. That sounded a whole lot better than Lou's Back Room in nearby Hallandale.

I left my apartment around 9:30 on a Saturday night in acid-washed Guess jeans, red earrings as big as boomerangs, and way too much Halston perfume. The parking lot at Shangri-La was jammed, with cars circling. Women were lined up at the door. Seeing the line, and knowing I'd have to walk up and join it, I almost did a U-turn for home. But the distance between me and that line needed to close. I found a parking spot and left the cardboard women in my back seat to find the real thing.

Monday morning, I was back at work.

Part of my job was going into stores and drugstores to make sure our products had strong shelf display. "Real estate is everything," my boss said about a hundred times. Most sales reps found store checks a task too menial. I loved arranging our bottles on the shelves and moving the other shampoos to the back of the denture section.

One day, down on the dusty bottom shelf with the other dog-brand hair care products, I saw a lone bottle of Clairol Herbal Essence, the swoon-inducing shampoo used by my fifth-grade teacher, Miss Mallory. I unscrewed the cap. I held the bottle up and put my nose close. I breathed in the juniper, birch, and pine.

CHAPTER 23

I dreamt about getting fired. It was blissful. Waking up was the nightmare. There had to be ways to get out of Revlon, short of death. Lyme disease required bed rest for several months with full pay. I considered the air force, like my brother, who lived on an air base near the French border and was dating a five-foot-nine German goddess. Maternity leave would get me eight weeks off work, but that would mean a baby. I met a woman and for a few weeks she made me forget my troubles until we had a big fight in my car on I-95 one night and she started throwing my cardboard Revlon women out the window.

Then, a friend offered me a two-month cat-sitting gig in an apartment on the beach in St. Pete. Another friend, Harper, who was the classical music critic at the *St. Petersburg Times*, encouraged me to apply for a job in the newsroom. It would be quite the salary hit. I'd be answering phones in the newsroom. Good enough for me! I quit Revlon the same day. I turned in the keys to my company car and got out of Fort Lauderdale so fast I left my eighty-two-year-old landlady twenty cases of hair care products in my living room.

I had another reason for returning to St. Pete. When I turned twenty-three, a birthday card from my mother appeared in my Fort Lauderdale mailbox:

> *Looking forward to you coming home so that we can have some time to re-establish ourselves as women.*

I read the words several times trying to figure out what she meant. Maybe my mother was willing to meet the twenty-three-year-old gay woman who happened to be her daughter.

THE *ST. Pete Times* was downtown amidst the green benches, deserted haberdashers, and Wig Villa. It was down the street from Webb's City, my old mermaid haunt. The newsroom was just as rundown, with stained carpet and ceiling tiles hanging low over the desks of dozens of reporters all trying to get to the bottom of things.

I started in Sports serving as an aide-de-camp to the paper's beloved sports columnist. He was a gentle bear with an encyclopedic knowledge of sports history that he kept to himself unless asked, and then in his shy Georgia manner he'd share what Jack Nicklaus told him at Pebble Beach in '72. I sat on the sports desk with about ten guys. They were the nicest people until they were on deadline, and then even the meekest pip-squeak would slam the phone down on the graphics department and scream, "Eat me." The next day they were back to their caring selves.

It hardly felt like work. I loved their company. They were hilarious nerdy widgets in golf shirts who thought they were studs. They had their own greeting. A guy would come on for his shift and someone would say, "How's it hanging?" The answer varied. "Exclusively to the left." Or, "Straight hang today." I had no idea what they were talking about.

One afternoon I was sitting in the pit with the other guys when my boss, the courtly sports columnist, walked past and I greeted him with, "Hi, Hubert, how's it hanging?" He paused mid-step, and then said, "Very well, thank you," and continued on to his office. The guys stifled their guffaws until his office door shut.

After six months in sports, I was promoted to answering phones on the city desk—the big leagues. From 4 to 11 p.m., I had a kook on hold on every line. Tipsters who had the inside dope on a stolen three-wheeler in their trailer court. Readers who wanted to let us know it was raining or ask what time *The Love Boat* came on TV. Around 9 the UFO sightings started to come in. I took down all the stories, filling notebook after notebook. Having someone listen made the callers feel as if they mattered; writing it all down did the same for me.

My favorite kook, my grandmother, called each night to get a bead on the day's news. She was still sending in her letters to the editor. They loved her down at the paper. I witnessed the unbridled glee of a copy editor who received one of my grandmother's letters. "What a nut job!" the guy called out across three desks. "Let's get this in ASAP."

Everyone in the newsroom leaned forward as they walked. The paper often put pictures of squirrels splashing in rain puddles on the front page of the metro section; at the same time, the Big Important Reporters flew off to meet secret sources at a Taco Bell off the Jersey Turnpike. One female reporter in her early sixties had a big Mary Tyler Moore flip and wore L'eggs pantyhose as she listened to FBI recordings. I'd never been part of something so important.

I was on the city desk one day when Harper came over. He asked if I wanted to write a record review. "For the paper?" I said, trying to keep my voice down because these people could be having lunch in the cafeteria and hear a dime drop in an elevator. "No, for *Highlights* magazine," he said. "Yes, for the paper."

TED GOT a better job offer in Delaware. My mother had become a principal by then, so she stayed in St. Pete. They planned to commute back and forth for a year. Halfway through the year, Ted called to say he wanted a divorce. I wasn't sad in the least. My mother was a bona fide wreck. She held it together for school, but after the last bell, she returned to her stupor of grief and crying in the frozen food section at the grocery store. The aloneness terrified her. She'd married a man she wasn't sure she loved to avoid being alone and old, and here she was, in her mid-fifties and alone.

She blamed herself; she'd been a terrible wife and there was no convincing her otherwise. Her grief surprised me; it surprised everyone because she'd made light sport of Ted since they married. His miserly habits and rare coin shows, his opera and velour bathrobe. Ultimately, her schtick was never about Ted but about her inability to love him.

My brother and I did an intervention of sorts. Jim was back in the country, and seeing her in a broken state unnerved him. It was nine o'clock on a Saturday morning. She wasn't reading the paper or making lists or starting a marinade for a dinner party that night. She was in bed, with the curtains closed, sealed off. Jim brought her coffee with the right amount of half-and-half. When that didn't excite her, I came back with two biscotti. Finally, Jim took her hand and held it in his catcher's mitt of a paw. "Mom, you've got *us*," he said. "Two wonderful kids."

A light flared in her eyes. "I wouldn't go *that* far," she said, giving Jim a cocked eyebrow. From there, little by little, she got better.

The first step was a cocker spaniel. She spent three hours at the pet store debating which dog to buy. "I didn't spend this long picking my second husband," she told the pet store employees.

SINCE SHE didn't have to go to gun shows on the weekend, I took her to drag brunches. Drag queens were naturally drawn to her, and she to them, maybe for their shared love of a good creamy foundation. Performers stopped by our table to see her do her Cruella de Vil eyebrow arch.

She was the principal of one of St. Pete's toughest middle schools. On Monday mornings, she woke up and did what she did best, and that was sitting in front of the bathroom mirror at 6 a.m. with a curling iron as she got ready for her show, the school day.

One afternoon, I dropped by her school to say hi. I saw her head sticking out of a dumpster behind the cafeteria. Maybe it was a hostage situation, so I ran to the dumpster. She was knee-deep in garbage in her Anne Klein blazer and gold earrings, sorting through lunch scraps and milk cartons. A boy from a violent home had accidentally tossed out his watch on his lunch tray and was terrified of a beating. I often teased my mother that school fed her performance streak. But in the dumpster, searching for a watch she would never find, her only audience was her squawking walkie-talkie on the ground.

On Sunday mornings, she called to go over my most recent story. She gave a full literary analysis to a ten-paragraph story on Madonna's rubber bracelets. She cut them out of the paper and highlighted her favorite lines. Off to the side were little handwritten "bravos." She did this year after year as the stories got longer, giving the same attention to a record review of the Go-Go's and a four-thousand-word piece about a police squad in a public housing project. She was proud of my newspaper job, but there was wistfulness there, too, a reminder of what she didn't do. It wasn't envy, just wistfulness, and I could read it in her eyes and it bummed me out.

I WAS covering a murder trial in Tampa when a reporter from New York or Chicago or somewhere asked me what was it like to actually live in Florida. He was a nice guy and not at all an asshole. He really wanted to know. "You don't find anything . . . unusual . . . that the dead guy is a carnival sideshow act known as Lobster Boy?"

I didn't. Florida was my normal. I'd lived my entire life within the same 250-mile radius. I wasn't desperate to escape. But the idea gnawed at me and I decided to apply for a year-long journalism fellowship at Harvard University.

Damie had moved into a nursing home when she was ninety, but she still had her marbles. I saw her two or three times a week, often crossing paths with my mother. We'd take Damie out in her wheelchair on a desolate St. Pete Sunday afternoon and abandon her in the middle of a crosswalk. My mother and I thought it was the funniest thing in the world. Damie put up with our hijinks and waited patiently for us to come get her. Back in her room, we drank milkshakes. "Look at us," Damie said with a smile. She gave us her typically self-deprecating assessment: "Three generations of losers."

I loved being in that club. Losers may have been overstating it, yet each of us felt the truth of it. I'd always had the feeling that I'd fallen short somehow.

There were twelve slots for the Harvard fellowship. I got one of them.

"A shampoo salesman at Harvard!" my mother said. "How 'bout that, Plant City girl."

As soon as I got settled in Cambridge, my mother bought a plane ticket to come see me. I wrote letters to her telling her about the classes I had with famous professors and how hard it was choosing which lecture to attend. Every day was like waking up in a casino for the mind with coins that poured down nonstop.

WHEN I heard my mother's voice on the phone, I knew something was wrong. My grandmother had pneumonia. She was alive when I got there. My mother was in a chair next to my grandmother's bed, holding a wadded-up tissue.

IT WAS hard to imagine a world without my whimsical, magical grandmother. For my sixth birthday, she gave me a View-Master and a slide of Pompeii with humans covered in lava. She paid me fifty cents for every Shakespeare sonnet I memorized out of one of her used paperbacks. I earned a dollar fifty and went back to Tarzan. She let me into her fantasy world and I was losing that, too.

The day after Damie died, my mother and I went to the funeral home to arrange her cremation. The funeral director took both of our hands and led us to a desk, where he carefully turned the pages of a huge book with pictures of urns, describing each one in minute detail. After about ten urns in, Mom turned to me and said, "Just put my ashes in a potted palm near the accessories counter at Macy's."

I worried about my mother, who had lost one more anchor. What would she do on Sunday afternoons if not visit Damie at the nursing facility? But my rich life in Cambridge was waiting.

I had never lived in snow. I walked home from lectures at the Kennedy School across a snowy Harvard Yard and stopped for french fries at Mr. Bartley's Burger Cottage. I would eat them in my mittens as I walked back to my attic apartment. One snowy night, five months after Damie died, I came home to nine messages flashing on my machine.

My mother had suffered a massive brain aneurysm during school lunch. She was fifty-six.

She died a day later, with me by her bedside and my brother stuck on a military transport flight from his air base in Turkey.

The funeral was at St. Paul's, our old Catholic school. There were four hundred mourners packed into the church, with an overflow crowd outside on the steps. My mother had worked in the school system for twenty-five years. Her former students came, teacher friends, the superintendent, the former superintendent, the woman who cleaned her house twice a month, her hairdresser, her dentist and his office staff, and reporters and editors from my newsroom.

"We are gathered here today for our sister Virginia," the elderly priest said, calling my mother by the wrong name.

Near the end of the service, the music director at Mom's middle school tapped her baton and the chorus sang an off-key version of "Like an Eagle" that brought the house down.

Death always bored my mother, but she would have appreciated the scene. Ted, my stepfather, was sitting in the back of the church. So was my father.

A DAY later, Dad reached out to me with a tenderness that was almost too intense to bear. "I know how much your mama meant to you and Dwight," he said. I worried that he sensed in the depths of my black heart that I wished he'd died and not my mother.

He was living at Gigi's old house in Plant City. The showy pink hibiscus shrubs were gone from the yard, but inside, nothing had moved an inch even though Gigi had been dead for years. Her white piano was still angled in the corner of the tiny living room like a formal Parisian salon. The pewter picture frames of Dad and Aunt Anne were in the exact same place on the exact same oak table next to the same wingback chair.

I went to see him, desperate for any scraps of information

about my mother. He knew things about her that no one else did. He sat patiently on an embroidered chair, answering questions about her that only an insider would know. All I had to do was ask a question. Details going back thirty years were at his fingertips. It was obvious that my sudden interest in him was transactional—I walked into his house with a notebook—but he'd take any pretense I was willing to give him if it meant spending time with me.

He told me about a date they had in Tallahassee, on a night they had gone to eat oysters in Apalachicola. On their drive back to FSU, a Kay Starr song came on the radio.

> *If I could hear no music*
> *If there could be no roses*

"John, please change the channel," my mother said.

My dad explained to me why. "Your mama said the song reminded her of her brother Percy's death and the terrible time around it." He described how my grandmother uprooted her three kids in search of medical care for Percy. It wasn't a story about determination, as I'd always imagined. Uncle Rod was fifteen at the time. "Uncle Roddy, they used him to drive them all over the country," Dad said. "And your mama, they farmed her out during that period." My mother was sent to live with various relatives in Brooklyn for weeks at a time. She was thirteen.

"Farmed out." That's the phrase that stuck with me.

I was too chicken to tell my father I was gay. I intended to, but at the end of my visit, I still hadn't done it. As we stood at the door saying goodbye, he jingled the coins in his pocket and I twisted the car keys in my hand. The moment came. I couldn't spit out the words.

My brother later said Dad probably figured as much.

MY FATHER was the one to indirectly raise the topic in a letter about a year after my mom died.

> As you know, I was raised in a more conservative time in regards to all aspects of life but as I grow older, I have grown more tolerant of things. As people age, they grow more mellow or more harsh in viewing the world.
>
> It would be nice to see or hear from you now and then—to have lunch, dinner or just drink a cup of coffee with you. I know you are on the fast track in a career and, also, have a personal life, but think about it.
>
> Love,
> Daddy

I took it as a green light to start anew with my father and called him. To show him I was no longer the child he remembered, and certainly not anyone who used the word "Daddy," I steamrolled over his suggestion of a simple cup of coffee and invited him to Bern's, the most expensive steakhouse in Tampa, my treat. Then I mentioned I'd like to bring my partner to dinner. He stammered, not knowing how to respond. After an awkward pause, he courteously replied. "That would be fine," he said.

It didn't occur to me that my father had not been to a restaurant that accepted reservations in two decades.

I realized it only when my partner and I walked into the restaurant that night, a place with red-velvet walls that was so baroquely obscene it was like being swallowed by a whale. There was no sign of my father. Fifteen minutes passed, then a half hour; then I started checking every room in the sprawling restaurant. He didn't own a cell phone and there was no way to reach him.

My father had been dry for twenty-five years, so I hadn't bothered to check the small dark cocktail lounge, but I doubled back, and there he was, in a khaki suit jacket, hunched over a highball glass.

"Dad?" I said, making sure it was club soda in his glass.

He turned around, agitated and sweating. His emphysema had gotten worse, and the drive to the restaurant in his old car in summer heat and rush-hour traffic nearly did him in. He'd been sitting there for an hour, waiting for me, convinced that I'd stood him up. He was unable to recover for the rest of the night. I wanted my partner to see an interesting man with a wide knowledge about many things, but he was withdrawn, even sullen. He was flustered by the waiter and irritated by my efforts to get the conversation going.

When would I ever learn that going to a steakhouse with my father never ended as I'd hoped. After that night, I didn't talk to him again for several years, partly mad and partly resigned to the fact that we would never get things right.

My brother told me that Dad brought up the night at the steakhouse a hundred times, wishing we could do it over.

I SAID goodbye to Florida and moved to Washington for work. Walking home in the cold on a winter night, I cursed the place and I cursed the know-it-alls who populated it. In friendly conversations, I'd refer to Washington, DC, as "up north" and be reminded by someone in a dry-cleaned shirt that Washington was south of the Mason-Dixon Line, so technically not "up north." They had their own unique way of setting you straight. "Let me tell you a fun story about Jeremiah Dixon," a guy said as he launched into his history lesson.

Suffering from a profound case of dislocation, I called my father. By then he was living in a low-income facility for the elderly in downtown Plant City. Aunt Anne was a resident there, too, still guzzling Co'Colas and looking at sewing patterns. Neither had ever remarried. They'd sold their thirteen acres of groves at Hopewell to a cousin, and when the funds ran out, they both moved into small apartments at the old folks' facility.

I visited him three times that year. He would answer the door, frail and tethered to an oxygen tank. We'd sit in his dim, concrete apartment. I would bring out my notepad to take notes, and he would bring his own. He always prepared questions for me, such as why did the press give former UN ambassador Jeane Kirkpatrick such a hard time.

When Dad was near the end, Jim called, and I got on the next flight to Florida. I got to the hospital just in time. Dad seemed to know I was there with a squeeze of the hand.

Before the funeral, my brother and I went to Bealls to buy Dad a nice white shirt to be buried in, since he had none. I followed my brother around the store like a child.

Jim knew the exact size Dad wore. He knew Dad would prefer a plain white shirt, the kind he had worn all his life. Jim was the one my father phoned in a panic at 2 a.m. saying his medication had been stolen, and Jim was the one who went right over and found the medication in the cushion of the recliner. When Aunt Anne's TV remote wasn't working, Jim drove over to change the batteries. I did nothing.

Jim still called me Sister. I called him Boy. But the man I followed around the store was nothing like a boy anymore.

The graveside service was at Plant City's oldest cemetery. Some of Dad's friends from high school and from his citrus days were there, including George LaMartin, the voice I'd heard on the CB radio when I'd ridden through the groves with my father. He was leathery and sunburned, the back of his neck crosshatched like a real citrus man. A big spray of roses was on top of my dad's casket, along with a few other vases of flowers sent by friends who hadn't seen him in years. Near the end of the service, the minister asked us all to form a circle and join hands to pray. I was half tuned out until I heard the word "daughter." My eyes jacked open.

Unbeknownst to me, the pastor had asked my brother if there was anything weighing on Dad's mind. This had happened at the hospital when Dad was hooked up to machines and close to the end, and Jim was exhausted. As a six-foot-six grown man, my brother was just as good-natured and kind as he had been in boyhood. Wanting to help the preacher out, Jim mentioned that his sister was gay and wasn't close with Dad, and this pained my father.

I was holding hands with a stranger next to a pile of fresh dirt when the pastor asked our heavenly father to deliver Brother John's daughter from homosexuality. I glared across the prayer circle at my brother, who was mouthing the words, "Oh, shit." He'd been preyed upon at a vulnerable moment. It was bad enough that the pastor dragged me into his theater of concern, but he did it to a dead man, who would not have approved of the message.

I WISHED I were the sort of person to go up to the minister afterward and tell him to kiss my lesbian ass. But it was Plant City. I guess I was Plant City. I hated to disappoint a religious zealot. I thanked the pastor for leading the service for my father.

CHAPTER 24

Almost nothing in Florida stays the way it was. It's bought, sold, paved over, and reimagined in a cycle that never quits. The landscape I saw through my father's windshield as a child has been so thoroughly erased I sometimes wonder if I made it up.

After the funeral, I drove out to Hopewell in a rental car. State Road 60 was now an onslaught of billboards for male hair-growth solutions, personal injury attorneys, and fat-vacuuming procedures. I thought of Aunt Dot posting her homemade signs for the fruit stand along the same road, how gaudy and urgent they seemed sticking up out of the wilderness. The clutter gave way to moss and two turns later I saw the towering live oaks of Hopewell. The place looked exactly the same. The same long driveway of crushed shells that my father drove up when he brought my mother home to meet his family. The same two houses at the end of the driveway that had been dragged from down the road by a team of mules a hundred years earlier.

It was all the same, as long as I used my hands as a telescope to look through.

The orange groves were gone. Sixty acres of Hull Groves, the trees that stretched out in the thousands behind the houses and around the houses, were gone. The dense hedges of shade and fragrance were now strawberry fields, with ten-inch-high plants that smelled like nothing.

The land was so open I could see a clothesline in the distance with white shirts on it.

The orange trees had been destroyed by a sickness that is carried in the wind. One tree gets sick and to prevent spreading, a hundred others around it are tagged for death until all must go. I watched a dying orange grove get turned up once. The sounds were awful. Grinding gears of backhoes and whining machinery, trees snapping and roots being ripped from the earth, and then quiet. The sudden brightness made it unrecognizable to anyone who knew it before.

Hopewell was like that. The clothesline in the distance felt like a taunt, daring me to conjure the place I remembered.

I remembered running through the groves the summer I was six. My father and I were in a big labyrinth of Valencia trees somewhere on the Ridge. We were parked in between the rows. I wandered away from the car to go scavenging. Every grove had secret things in it that didn't belong there. I'd found a lipstick case, a pocket-size Bible, shotgun shells, liquor bottles, bloody clothes, and fancy hair barrettes. Once I found the shed skins of a diamondback rattlesnake that uncoiled to a length of five feet. On this particular day, I spotted a white plastic strip on the ground. It was a hospital bracelet and someone had used their teeth to bust out of it. I dropped the chewed-up bracelet and ran for my life.

I imagined an escaped convict or a lunatic loose in the grove and that he was behind me, getting closer. I ran in one direction and then another. I couldn't find my father's car. A vulture's shadow spread around me in the sand as it flew over. "Dad!" I yelled, gasping for air. Each row was the same identical hedge taking me deeper into the dark maze. Please God, don't let me die in an orange grove.

Then I heard the low deep sound of the pickers' voices talking to each other from their ladders. I ran toward the voices that would save me.

ACKNOWLEDGMENTS

Thank you to my agent, Tina Bennett, for her tenacious support and unbreakable faith. She was always up ahead with the lantern, reading pages, sending thoughts, and certain of the journey.

My brother, Jim Hull, gave his guidance and help at every step. He is the master historian of our growing up; his insights appear on every page of this book, his light shines far beyond. Thank you, Brother.

I'm grateful to the resident experts at Hopewell for their deep knowledge of land and family: Tom and Andi Hull, Susie Fleck, Caroline Hull, and Jimmy Hull.

Special thanks to the following people for sharing their memories, knowledge, and willingness to dig through storage lockers, old yearbooks, and letters bundled together in rubber bands: my wise friend Candy Owens, Marvin and Elsa Kahn, Patti Crawford, Wanda Whitehouse, Marge Jernigan, Carole Goad at the Sebring Historical Society, and Shelby Bender at the East Hillsborough Historical Society.

At Henry Holt, thank you to John Sterling, Barbara Jones, and most of all to my editor Caroline Zancan, who deserves a shoebox full of large bills for the patience and care she gave to the manuscript, also to Lori Kusatzky and Chris O'Connell for their invaluable help. Grateful thanks to Anne Sibbald and Bennett Ashley at Janklow & Nesbit for their good counsel.

Generosity came from all corners—the *Washington Post*, the American Academy in Berlin, Steve Coll, Don Graham, Dana Priest, Kelley Benham French, Elena Blum, Eileen McClay, Angela Hull, and friends of the tribal sort who provided their formidable talents to read and reread piles of words: David Maraniss, Katherine Boo, Tom French, Paul Tash, Kathryn Kross, Sonya Doctorian, and the chief untangler Melissa Bell, who made things right and knew how to shut the club down.

The search for home ended when I met Ines Pohl, my tall transatlantic soulmate whose heart and spirit could fill an ocean.

ABOUT THE AUTHOR

Anne Hull is a Pulitzer Prize–winning journalist who spent nearly two decades as a reporter at the *Washington Post*. She is a fifth-generation Floridian who started her newspaper career at the *St. Petersburg Times* (now the *Tampa Bay Times*). She lives in Washington, DC.